LORD I BELIEVE

▽ ▽ ▽ ▽ ▽

April 2006 A gift from crystal rhodes.

AUSTIN FARRER

▽ ▽ ▽ ▽ ▽

LORD
I BELIEVE

Suggestions for
Turning the Creed into Prayer

1 9 8 9

Cowley Publications
Cambridge, Massachusetts

This Cowley edition of *Lord I Believe* is the first U.S. release of this title, and is a reprint of the book's second edition, revised and expanded, published in 1958 by Faith Press in Great Britain.

International Standard Book Number: 0-936384-70-0
Library of Congress Number: 88-39444

Library of Congress Cataloging-in-Publication Data
Farrer, Austin Marsden.
    Lord I believe / Austin Farrer.
        p. cm.
    ISBN 0-936384-70-0 : $6.95
    1. Apostles' Creed—Meditations. 2. Rosary. I. Title.
BT993.2.F37 1989
238'.11—dc19   88-39444

Cowley Publications
980 Memorial Drive
Cambridge, MA 02138

A TRIBUTE TO AUSTIN FARRER

In the opinion of some, Austin Farrer is the one Genius produced by the Church of England this century. His Genius consists of a unique interpenetration of the spiritual, theological and the poetic. What is surprising about a person whose mind was uncompromisingly intellectual is that his genius flowered in his more popular writings. It is very good news that *Lord I Believe* is now available for a new readership. Farrer's meditations on the fundamentals of faith stimulate our mind, arouse our imagination and warm our heart.

—Richard Harries
Bishop of Oxford

About sixteen years ago Austin Farrer re-converted me—not just with his profoundly original philosophical apologetic but with his sermons and devotional works. Here he proved that faith as a lived relationship with the Triune God is after all possible for late twentieth-century intellectuals and that the ancient doctrine of the Creed is still a faith to be lived. How good it is, therefore, that *Lord I Believe* is at last to be available again, and this time to American readers! For these "Suggestions on Turning the Creed into Prayer" give the practical answer to the century's most sustained inquiry into the action of God. The place where we can best know God's effective action is in our intentional cooperation with his grace. Prayer is the place to begin, and the place to begin prayer is with meditation on the Creed. Whoever takes up Farrer's meditations may therefore hope that the action of prayer will become the very action of God lived through us into the world.

—Ed Henderson
Department of Philosophy
Louisiana State University

CONTENTS

CHAPTER I

On Praying the Creed

PRAYER and dogma are inseparable. They alone can explain each other. Either without the other is meaningless and dead. If he hears a dogma of faith discussed as a cool speculation, about which theories can be held and arguments propounded, the Christian cannot escape disquiet. 'What are these people doing?' he will ask. 'Do not they know what they are discussing? How can they make it an open question what the country is like, which they enter when they pray?'

To put the matter the other way round, suppose that our believing friends express bewilderment over the use and function of prayer. Shall we not ask them what they imagine their belief to be about? They may say it gives them a true description of the world in which they are called upon to act. Certainly; but not, surely, an obvious description, nor a description which, once learnt, continues steadily to illuminate the realities of life. I believe in God the Father Almighty, Maker of heaven and earth; and yet I may run this pen over the paper all morning without a thought for that infusion of the divine likeness into flesh, which makes intelligence act in my fingers, and my fingers drive the pen. I believe in Jesus Christ, born, suffering, risen; yet I may leave the desk for the table, and find in my fellow diners the objects of my rivalry or the sources of my amusement, but never see the Christ in their hearts, or acknowledge in mine the Christ who goes out to meet them.

Our creed shows us the truth of things, but when shall we attend to the truth it shows? The life of the world is a strong conspiracy not of silence only but of blindness concerning the side of things which faith reveals. We were born into the conspiracy and reared in it, it is our second nature, and the Christianity into which we are baptized makes little headway against it during the most part of our waking hours. But if we go into our room and shut the door, by main force stop the wheel of worldly care from turning in our head, and simply recollect; without either vision or love barely recall the creed, and re-describe a corner of our world in the light of it; then we have done something towards using and possessing a truth which Jesus died to tell, and rose to be.

We have done something, but the truth of Christ is living truth, and will do more. Truth will do much for us unknown to us, clearing our eyes and purging our heart, when we seem to be observing the merest custom of prayer. But often truth will shine and strike us : 'What have I been thinking? What have I been missing? How could I be such a fool, to forget Jesus in my friends, and to see them as so many claimants, rivals, bores, obstacles, instruments? Such a fool (but it was worse than folly) as to turn steadily from the will of God, which alone is my bread and sunlight and breathable air, and fill my hours with self-seeking?' Then we are broken-hearted and then we rejoice; broken-hearted at what we have refused to see, but rejoicing more, because we see it; and we go on in our prayer to express some rudiments of love for our neighbour and our God, and to devise some way for giving that love effect.

Prayer is the active use or exercise of faith; and the creed defines the contours of that world on which faith trains her eyes. These statements are, or ought to be, platitudes. No dogma deserves its place unless it is prayable, and no Christian deserves his dogmas who does not pray them. But if so, what are we to say to that high doctrine of the saints, which tells us when we pray to aim at utter simplicity, stilling first our imagination, then our thought, and adhering by naked will to a God we forbear to conceive? How strange this sounds ! The saints who teach the doctrine are Christian saints, and they tell us, as any Christian must, that our salvation hangs on the revelation Christ achieved, and of which the shape is given us in the creed. They wish us to treasure the dogmas which our teachers laboured so hard to bring home to us; they wish us to be no less patient ourselves in handing them on to others. Can it then really be the intention of the saints that we should hold our treasures as a miser holds his wealth, and make no use of them? The sublime doctrines of our faith cannot affect our lives except through prayer, and yet, if we are to take the maxims of the saints at their face value, must not we make it our whole endeavour to forget the doctrines when we pray?

The paradox is not really so sharp as it sounds. The high instruction of the saints is not for beginners. It is addressed to those who have done the necessary work of preparation, and made the creed their own through much reflection on it. An analogy may help those of my readers who have had the experience to which it refers. Those who fall in love may seem to themselves, and especially after the event, to have been simply swept away by the beauty they have seen. And it may sometimes be so, indeed most probably so if bodily beauty alone has captured the heart. But if we have loved the person, or the soul, we have loved what cannot be seen, either with the eyes or with any other organ of sense. Our vision of the person is a knowledge of their thoughts and ways, acquired piecemeal from their conduct and brought together into a single view. And this bringing together is something that we do, it does not happen of itself. If we remember carefully we may recall a time of intense mental activity, when we were comparing the actions and opinions, the habits and expressions of our friend, and trying to make them fit. We thought we knew the person more vividly than we had ever known any one, and then found ourselves suddenly baffled; a stranger stood before us, and we began all over again.

There was such a time, but it came to an end at last, and we knew our friend, not as God knows his creature, but as well as one creature hopes to know another. To bring our friend before us we no longer needed to make explorations in the field of memory. We had only to say the name 'John' or 'Mary,' or whatever it might be, to find ourselves at a point of mental vision like the convergence of the avenues in an old-fashioned park. As though the very word 'Mary' or 'John' were a statue or a pillar marking the place where all our vistas crossed; we could rest upon it and enjoy our mental paradise in peace. We had no need to explore the avenues to their ends, we could see down them from the place where we were, and recognize what we saw, for we had often been there to look. Even to shift our eyes too curiously from one line of vision to another would have disturbed our intimacy with the spirit of the garden; it was better to let the scene flow in upon us, and not to know what our eyes were at; to dwell with quiet affection on the beloved name and let the fragrance of the person gather round it.

Now to apply the comparison to the thing : there was a time when the lover of God, like the lover of Mary or of John, was putting together his knowledge of God, gathered piecemeal from reflection on the ways and works of God, as they are delineated in the creed and recognized in life. But again, there was a time, not so soon reached but reached at last, when the knowledge of God gathered round the Name of God; and though it remained often profitable to explore one by one his glorious works, and necessary often to wrestle in particular with the interpretation of his ways, yet it was good, and indeed best of all, to be quiet at the place from which sprang all the paths of light and name the Name of God, giving up the soul entirely to that unity of all perfection for which the Name had come to stand.

The saint is happy to be able to do this, and can do it, because he formerly explored and meditated the compass of the creed. There he marked out the widely spread circumference of God's revealing action, from which he has since moved in to find the centre. We, perhaps, are still plotting the circle of our faith, or have not even properly begun. If so, let us not leave off at the call of a false mysticism which mistakes the end for the beginning, moves inward from the tracings of thought and imagination before anything has been either imagined or thought, and dwells in a centre which is as yet the centre of nothing.

Comparisons of human things with divine, the more vivid they are, the more they mislead us; and the analogy we draw between the love of God and the love of our fellow-man fails at a capital point. Although the idea of a person whom we love speaks in a name, and lives in our heart, it speaks with no voice and lives with no life of its own. Like the image in our eyes when we see, the idea in our mind moves and acts by reflection only of the person it mirrors. For the friend whom we love is outside us and cannot, except by a poetic fiction, be said to inhabit our mind, even when our thoughts are full of nothing else. If I speak to the idea in my heart, I speak to a puppet who cannot answer me, except through a trick of ventriloquism on my own part. If the answers are such as the real person would give, that is because I know the person and judge rightly of what I know. It is true that the images of our friends grow and change powerfully in our minds apart from any influence from without; but then it is our minds that grow and alter, and the images of our friends only in so far as they have become incorporated with our minds. We mark our hearts with beloved names as boys mark trees with them; the names grow and change their shape with the growth of the tree.

In so far as we owe the image or idea of God to our Christian upbringing, it is, like the images of our friends, scored on our minds from without, and grows as our minds grow. But God is what our friends are not—he is the ground of our being, and principle of our growth; so that the way in which his idea develops in us becomes his own concern, for our whole growth is his concern. It is possible, then, for him to live and act in our idea of him as no friend can do, and our faith trusts him to do precisely this—to become in us an active, living truth. So, when we speak to him under the form of our idea of him, we do not address a puppet of our own, nor do we ventriloquize the puppet's answers. No; if there are any puppets in the case it is we, with all our ideas, who are the puppets—puppets in the hand of God; and our prayer is this, that God, fashioning our thought and especially our thought of God, would make his handiwork speak with his voice. And this he will do, if he so pleases, not by a conjuror's pretence but out of our own throats. What the ventriloquist feigns the Creator performs. He who has moulded man from clay breathes into his nostrils the Holy Ghost and man becomes a living soul, especially in that part of him which is his thought of God. When I pray, let my heart ask God to speak through my heart, that my prayer, continued by his inspiration, may become the answer to itself.

Though God be in me, yet without the creed to guide me I should know neither how to call upon God, nor on what God to call. God may be the very sap of my growth and substance of my action; but the tree has grown so crooked and is so deformed and cankered in its parts, that I should be at a loss to distinguish the divine power among the misuses of the power given. Were I to worship God as the principle of my life, I should merely worship myself under another name, with all my good and evil. So I take refuge in that image of God which we have described as branded from outside upon the bark. Here is a token I can trust, for he branded it there himself; he branded it on the stock of man when he stretched out his hands and feet and shed his precious blood. The pattern of the brand was traced on me by those who gave the creed to me; God will deepen it and burn it into me, as I submit my thoughts to him in meditation.

I may pray for God to act in me by shaping his idea in me, but he, the living God in me, is not the idea but the power who shapes it. When I speak to God I fix my eyes on my idea of God and do not, in practice, distinguish it from him. Yet I cannot always shut out the truth—no idea of God is God; and there is a gulf, a break, a leap of the mind as, turning from the visible God to the invisible, it rejects the image it contemplates. 'O God' we may say 'I have been tracing your image. It was given and imprinted by you, but you it was not. You are the free omnipotence who make all images and are confined in none of them, nor will I limit you by any. Be yourself in your own way through my heart and in my heart; why should I be concerned to figure how you work or what you are? I throw myself back into the claypit from which you took me, to be fashioned again. I surrender my spirit to the God who gave it; quicken me with such life as it pleases you to breathe.'

What is divine about the mystical saints is what God does

with them when they have discreated themselves thus and put themselves back into God. Of that divine action in the saints there are several stages and degrees, which they have employed all their subtlety in trying to describe. They have also left us their accounts of the states and conditions of the soul which lay it most open to God, and the methods and courses of life by which such states are to be approached. Such is the high doctrine of mystical prayer, something far beyond us, and about which nothing will be said in this book. It is enough for us to consider two points which we have already touched, two renunciations which are made in more ordinary prayer.

First, we renounce the detailed consideration of God, all running to and fro of the mind over his nature or his ways, and let our knowledge gather quietly round his Name, content to dwell upon it or to make simple acts of affection towards it. Second, we reject everything that has gathered there, however unobtrusively and tranquilly it is present to us, and appeal from the picture to the Painter, asking to be paint under his brush rather than eyes before his finished portrait.

These two renunciations are not peculiar to the saints, or to souls advanced in prayer, but are profitable to everyone who meditates. The question is, When should they be made? Those who are at work on fundamentals, praying the dogmas of the creed and the mysteries of the gospel, should always hope to make the first renunciation before they rise from their knees, loving in the unity of his Name the God whom they have considered in the variety of his ways. Those who have done some of the preparatory work may often begin, and not end, with this renunciation, putting consideration aside and directly invoking a God who is sufficiently present to them by his Name alone. The truths which gather round the Name swarm unbidden from the caverns of their memories, they are awakened by the words of a book or the voice of a preacher. There is no need to go forth and collect them; the soul may go on quietly to bless the Name of God.

As to the second renunciation, it is often not necessary that we should set ourselves to make it, but only as we may be moved.

But when we seem to be hearing our own voice, or are distressed by the artificiality of the thoughts we build or the sentiments we express, then at all events the second renunciation is a blessed refuge, and a means of turning the unprofitableness of our prayer to positive advantage. 'O God, all that I tell you about yourself is empty and false, but what does it matter? You are no set of words, you are the living God. I do not grasp you, but you grasp me and will not let me go. You are here, or rather, you are that place where I am when I say that I am here. I am with you and you are yourself, and for what else should I care? I cannot think of you, but you can think in me, or keep silence in me; above all, you can love in me.'

Renunciations are meaningless when there is nothing to renounce. Before we renounce the use of intellect and imagination we must use them well, we must meditate the creed. And those who have in some fashion mapped the country of their faith will not find that they have taken their bearings once and for all, or that they can, without further looking about, move single-mindedly towards the Centre. They must return often to their starting point and work in afresh from the circumference. For no spiritual truth, however fundamental, is once and for all acquired like gold locked in a safe. We think it is there—'That certainty is mine for good,' we say. But when we look for it, either it has vanished or it is no longer gold. It has turned as dull and soft as lead, and must be transmuted back to gold by the alchemy of living meditation.

The chapters which follow handle certain essential doctrines not in the actual form of prayer but in the attitude of one who means to pray, and so perhaps my readers will be ready to use the prayers appended to them. Written prayers must, of course, be said and not read, said slowly and with full intention; and if, having said them once, we seem not to have said what is in them, we can say them over again, and as often as they continue to serve us. And one way of making what we have called the 'first renunciation' is to continue saying a very simple formula over and over, until it becomes a mere support for the mind in loving God; as when S. Francis (by his own confession) spent the night saying 'Deus meus et omnia,' 'My God and my all.'

CHAPTER II

I believe in God the Father and in his only Son our Lord and in the Holy Ghost

THE Trinity cannot be explored except from the centre. And what is the centre? It is the Love of God. The name of Love has been fearfully profaned, and yet no other name will do. If, for example, we were content to contemplate the *benevolence* of God, we should not open up the region in which the Trinity is revealed, but only if we go beyond benevolence into love. Benevolence may be no more than a general and diffused well-wishing; love requires that a person should be infinitely prized. A headmaster might be sincerely benevolent, and not love a single one of his pupils; and that, perhaps, would be an ideal state of affairs. A father who was benevolent to his family and loved none of his children would not have done so well. The welfare state is a moral possibility if its officials are predominantly benevolent, but we do not expect them to love us.

In mentioning the welfare state we have hit upon a point of some religious importance, for the influence of political organization on religious feeling has been at all times profound. When we had absolute monarchy we had a theology of divine sovereignty; now we have welfare politics our religion is divine benevolence. It is instinctive in us to think of God's power as taking over where human power leaves off, as caring for the intimate distresses which no public officer relieves, controlling dangers no police can master, and, where the state hospital is defeated at last, raising the dead. But God's kingdom is not paternal government. Paternal government is only a bastard sort of fatherliness, and God is a true father so far as loving his children goes.

And that is easily said. It is easy to tell ourselves a tale about God's love for us, another thing to receive his love and reciprocate it, as it was Moses' privilege to do, when God is said to have

17

spoken with him as a man speaks with his friend, face to face and without disguises. A man's face lights up the face of his friend, and Moses' face shone, reflecting that countenance which is the Light of the world. Moses was remembered by Israel not as a man who spoke of divine love edifyingly, but as a man to whom divine love spoke effectively, so that he answered that love, reflecting it back upon God in prayer, and outwards in devotion to mankind.

Why talk about Moses, who has been stylized into a myth by remote tradition, and not about Christian saints, whose histories are more exactly recorded? We would indeed talk about the saints if we were citing evidence, but at present we are doing no such thing. We are forming a picture to fix our minds on, and the pictorial qualities of the ancient figure are striking enough. And for the same reason let us, while we are about it, recall another antique personage. If God is said to have spoken with Moses as a man speaks to his friend, he is said to have honoured Abraham with the actual title: 'Abraham, my friend,' says the divine voice; his friend because he was admitted to his confidence. 'Shall I hide from Abraham,' said the Lord God, 'the thing that I do, seeing that I know him?' So Abraham was lifted into the counsels of God; and we read in the touching simplicity of the ancient story how, in the guise of a traveller unknown, God came upon Abraham sitting by his tent door in the cool of the day. Abraham, showing all hospitable kindness, entertained not only angels, but his Creator unawares, and had such discourses at his table as are to form the everlasting bliss of heaven.

What Genesis sets forth in the vividness of the picture is to be enjoyed by every Christian in the reality of spirit. God makes every one of us his friend, he sets us at his table, he shares his thought with us, he shows us his kindness, he puts an infinite price upon our love. Many truths of religion will bear endless meditation, but this above all; we can recall it as often as we pray, that God holds our love for him incomparably more dear than we hold the love of those who are dearest to us. Nothing moves our penitence more than to recognize that we have withheld what God desires and ourselves despised what he prizes most; nothing calls out our adoration more than a love which, knowing us to the bottom, continues to care for us under all our self-obsession and frivolity. It would be a great thing if we could love any single person as we love ourselves, but we cannot love even ourselves as our Creator loves us.

Friendship involves some kind of an equality, or, if not an equality, then an equalization. To make a friend of a child I must both be a child to him and also treat him as a grown person. God both descends to us, dealing humanly with his human creatures, and also lifts us to himself. It is by conversing with us that he brings us into conversation. There would be no light to shine back from Moses' face into the eyes of God, had Moses not received the shining of those heavenly eyes upon his own; no intercessions for Sodom in the mouth of Abraham, but that God provoked him into speech by first showing him the counsels of his judgment; no confidence to pray in any Christian heart, were it not warmed by the promises of mercy in Christ Jesus. To pray is to give God back the mind of God, coloured with our own. But we must first be given the mind of God, thoughts and concerns from a level above mortality.

God equalizes us with himself in the sense that he makes us party to a friendship with himself, but the equalization equalizes sheer inequalities. A man may make a friend of a child, some even say of a dog or of a horse, and such an affection may be stronger than friendship; but friendship it is not, in the strict sense of the word; at the most it is a special extension of friend-ship, and friendship would never have received a name if this were all the friendship that there was. By making a friend of a child we extend to him what belongs properly to our equal, and by making friends of us our Father and our God extends to us by a stretch incomparably wider what belongs uniquely to his co-equal Son. If God's love for us were all the love there was, then divine love would never have been. It is only because divine love has a natural object that it overflows to embrace an adopted object. We are the children of God by adoption, the eternal Son of God is Son by nature.

Human friendship, belonging to our equals, can be extended to children, but there is a special case of such extension to which the name 'extension' most properly applies. I mean when my friendship for children is part of, an extension of, my friendship for their parent, when my friendship for him or her embraces them. There is an even more special case when the friendship we are thinking of is between my wife and me (for surely married affection is friendship, though it is also more). Then the children are specially hers, and yet I have (as the common saying goes) given them to her. And so she comes before me as one who says, 'I and the children you have given me,' not wishing to be loved apart from the children. The Epistle to the Hebrews puts almost those very words into the mouth of Christ. Our Redeemer is as one who says : 'I and the children whom God has given me.' For the heavenly Father has given Christians to Christ, though not, of course, in the way in which a husband gives children to his wife; we are not speaking of a sexual relationship, however spiritualized. Nevertheless, Christ, like the woman we were thinking of, comes before the Father with us his children, as though unwilling to be loved by him, unless his love is extended to us. But what fear is there that it will not be so extended, considering that the Father has given us to his Son?

The love whereby our divine Father loves us is an actual part of the one love with which he loves his eternal Son, for God is one and his love is one piece. He could not be one unless his love were one, for he *is* love, says S. John, and only if there is one love can there be one God. So all the gifts of the Father's love to Christ are in a manner extended to Christians. 'Thou art my beloved Son, in thee I am well pleased' is an oracle of love that speaks to sinners, because they are among the number of whom Christ says : 'I and the children whom God has given me.'

'To know Christ is to know the benefits we derive from him,' says an old theologian. What benefit do we chiefly derive from him? The heavenly sonship which overflows from him to us. And how do we know him from that benefit? We see that what we have in part and by adoption he has by nature and in fullness, the pure and simple sonship is his. We do not best understand the Divine Father and the Divine Son by drawing analogies from human sons and human fathers, but by a method more real and more direct—that is, from experiencing divine sonship extended to ourselves.

But, having grasped the similarity, we must go on to seize the difference : the Son of God differs infinitely from us, his sonship from ours. It is usual to say that, whereas God *made* us, he begot his Son, but that is little better than a textbook formula. It draws a distinction, it does nothing to explain it. For we were not made, as we understand making, nor was he begotten, as we understand begetting. He was not begotten, for he was begotten in no womb, and we were not made, for we were made of no material. Both the only-begotten Son and we, the many spirits created, depend and derive wholly from the Father of all. The Eternal Son is utterly derived, utterly dependent, but he is the full expression of his Father's nature and being, and, therefore, not less in nature or glory than the Father who begets him. The Son also is Eternal God, for otherwise the Father's act of begetting would be imperfect, he would not beget what is best or worthiest of himself. The Son has nothing that he does not derive from the Father, but he derives from the Father all the Father has to give. Were he not equal with the Father, he would lack the capacity to receive all that the Father has the bounty to bestow. His love, like ours, is a response and a reciprocation; and no spirit lower than God can reciprocate all the love of God. He depends on the Father not for less than we do, but for infinitely more. Like us, he depends on the Father for all things. We receive from the Father all we are, he alone receives from the Father all the Father is.

We were thinking just now of Moses, and the shining of his face by reflection of divine radiance. But what a narrow glass is the up-turned face of Moses to reflect the glory of the Light that warms the world! Only the face of God reflects the face of God, there alone is converse in true equality, and eyes that answer eyes with a perfect intelligence. S. Paul, interpreting for us the shining of Moses' face, says that the God who inflows as light on Moses is the Holy Ghost. The apostle's interpretation is true to our experience; if we answer divine love it is by divine inspiration. But how little is there in us for the divine Spirit to inspire! The Holy Ghost is measured in us by the narrowness of our vessel, to the Eternal Son he gives himself without measure. The Son does not measure the Spirit by limiting him, he perfectly expresses him by perfectly receiving him. Holy Ghost means the divine life communicated or bestowed. Holy Ghost has no being except in another; the first and proper being of the Holy Ghost is in the Eternal Son.

What! Does the Eternal Son himself need to be inspired? If he is to answer his Father's love, cannot he answer of himself? The objection is a transposition into highest heaven of the famous English opinion that dependence on God is a weakness, that it would be better to be self-reliant. But Christianity leaves no place for the arguments of pride, least of all in the perfection of the Godhead. The Son delights to receive everything from his Father, and to draw all that is good from the only source of good. To answer the Father's love without the Father's inspiration would not (even if it were possible) be a heightening of bliss, but quite the reverse, for to be filled with God is exactly what we desire, or should desire; so what would be the blessedness of cutting off the channel? And heaven differs from earth chiefly in this, that the blessed are more completely dependent on God's inspiration than we are.

So there are two acts of God the Father, neither conceivable without the other—to beget and to bestow: to beget the Son, to bestow on him the Holy Ghost. Both acts are perfect : what is begotten is God, and what is bestowed is equally God. The divine Persons do not lack perfection by needing one another, for what they require they eternally possess. The Father does not lack for the expression of his Fatherhood, he expresses it perpetually in his Son. The Son lacks nothing of the Father's inspiration, since he has the Holy Ghost. The Spirit is not imperfectly real through being the completion of another's life; he enjoys perfection in being perfectly bestowed on a perfect recipient by a perfect giver. Here are not three Gods; here is one Godhead which can be what it essentially is, a society of Love, only through distribution in three Persons.

In the pursuit of such high mysteries our thought is lost; and yet the Trinity is no mere conjecture about the heart of Heaven. The Trinity is both the meaning and the setting of that love which the Father has actually bestowed upon us. We need have nothing to do with the Trinity as a cool speculation about the necessary nature of the Godhead; it would be idiocy to place such confidence in theological reasonings as to evolve it by rational argument. The Trinity is revealed to Christians because they are taken into the Trinity, because the threefold love of God wraps them round, because it is in the Trinity they have their Christian being. Every time I worship or pray or make the least motion of the heart towards God, I stand with the divine Son in face of the divine Father, the mantle of his sonship spread around me, and the love of the Father overflowing from him to me in the grace of the Holy Ghost.

A Christian who talks like this does not talk comfortably. His being in the Trinity is his Christian existence; it is the unspeakable gift of God's mercy to him. But all the gifts of God judge us as fast as they save us. It is the depth of my condemnation that I so meanly use the infinite generosity of God. And yet God's gifts save us as fast as they judge us, or they would not be gifts; his mercy prevails.

God above me, Father from whom my being descends, on whom my existence hangs, to whom I turn up my face, to whom I stretch out my hands :

God beside me, God in a man like me, Jesus Christ in the world with me, whose hand lays hold of me, presenting me, with yourself, to God :

God within me, soul of my soul, root of my will, inexhaustible fountain, Holy Ghost :

Threefold Love, one in yourself, unite your forces in me, come together in the citadel of my conquered heart.

You have loved me with an everlasting love. Teach me to care.

CHAPTER III

I believe in God Almighty, maker of heaven and earth

I GO down to my garden. My work is behind the season, the planting is urgent. While the planting has lagged, the weeds have grown, and the hoe is needed everywhere. Where shall I begin? The time I have this afternoon is so short. I rather think . . . Ah, there's a rustling in the fish-net which is supposed to cover the currants. Come out, you little wretch! Look, I have lifted the net for you. What, you won't? Then I must pretend to catch you. Here comes my hand. Not that way, foolish bird, what's the use of pushing into the mesh? Oh, I see, you have wound yourself in it. What have you done to yourself? You must have been struggling there for hours. I can't see how the mesh goes, it has cut so deep into you under the feathers; and how am I to tackle the knots round the wiry hooks of your claw? Anyhow there is nothing to be done until I have first freed your left wing. Don't struggle so, and don't look at me with such an eye. Oh, I see, round your neck, too, the mesh quite buried in your feathers; I strangle you when I pull on the twine to loosen your wing.

I sit down to the delicate puzzle, laying the thrush and the border of the net in my lap. My heart leaps as though my life were at stake. I am terrified, the sweat drips from my face. After twenty minutes of agonized endeavour I remember my knife. I cut the net to pieces and let the bird go. So there is my gardening: nothing planted out and my net rent. By the time I have patched it up with string I shall have to go.

Well, little bird, I had no notion of caring for you, and if I had turned my eyes half aside and knocked you on the head, I should have thought it reasonable enough. Which is worth more, a thrush's life or an afternoon's work? Where is the pair of scales in heaven or earth which will weigh them against each other : a fragment of my world against the whole of yours? For you, too, are a little world, an entire creation. When you fall to the earth something better than a star, a life is quenched; you do not fall without the will of our Father in heaven.

What a summary you are, when I consider you, of his creative skill. Your happy singleness of life holds together such a complexity of parts. You mean to go, and go in one continuous motion, scarcely knowing whether you run or fly, and never considering that you have wings or feet, until both are tangled in the net and you feel the difference of pain. As to the minute parts of which your legs and shoulders are composed, you have no sense of them, still less of the parts of which those parts are formed, and these again of others, unimaginably fine and small. Yet of all these you are the living summary, and not only of such actual constituents, but of the history which brought them together, developed them and disposed them in order. Where did your history begin? It lengthens as I look at it, and goes back behind every beginning that I hope to fix. Before you sprang from your parents, or any thrushes from other thrushes, the race itself grew from another, and that from another in turn. And all this history of growth has been conditioned by the general nature of the world; it has taken direction from numberless particular events which our speech would call matters of chance.

In so wide a survey I am lost. Let me return to you who so disturbed the rhythm of my heart. Those who have made themselves intimate with your kind say that you are each individual, as it were an elementary person. You have your own faces, your own characters, your own loves. You can be valued distinctly by those who know you, each for a unique and incommunicable charm. What has diversified you from the others, and made you yourself? You grew in a nest built in a particular tree, from which a certain view of things was in prospect. Your parents had a certain way with you, so had each of your fellow-nestlings. The sky of that spring had its own pattern of cloud and sunshine. When you were fully-grown, you found a mate, not like any other's mate. You have had various fortunes; I have frightened you almost to death, perhaps more than once. And so you are what you are.

You are what you are, and God has made you so. But how, when I consider the making, am I to apportion the parts of his creation and his providence, or draw the line between them? He did not first make finished works, and then direct their interplay. It is by governing the interplay of many elements that he has finished his works. If I consider that without something there to start with, there would be nothing to interplay under the direction of providence, then I put creation at the beginning. But when I consider that without the providential interplay no work receives a character or becomes a finished thing, then I put creation at the end. It is only a choice of words; whichever I say, it remains that providence and creation are inseparable.

In such a line of reflection there lies, surely, the promise of escape from nets in which thought flutters only to become the worse involved. Who has not wrestled with the riddle of providence, and asked how accident and disaster can be such close rivals to providential care? We are left uncertain whether to assert a providence or not. But if I confine providence within the lines of creation, I am freed from this perplexity. For it is certain to me that God has made many excellent creatures, and that without a providential control over an infinity of circumstances he could not have made them (or at any rate, did not; what he could have done is not for me to say). Equally it is certain, and I have never doubted it, that it does not belong to the nature of the bodily creatures to be exempt from harm or always to endure, but to be frail and perishable. God has made them so, and I should think it fantastic to challenge his choice in having so made them. I know very well that the thrush I have released with all this trouble may fly straight into another net and hang himself, or fall victim to the cat next door who wages so skilful a war on robber birds and robber mice. It will remain true that infinite providence went to the making of the bird, as also to the making of every other creature. The creatures are subject to flaws and tragedies, but apart from providence, there would be no creatures. God's providence is exerted in the line of his creative purpose, and in accordance with the nature of the world he makes. When final tragedy puts an end to the whole physical scene, it will remain that the hand which wrote the drama has concluded it, and that every character has had his appointed entry and exit. And if we are surprised that God should lavish infinite care on transitory things, it may be because we forget that he is God. To us small exertions are a taking of pains, but to him infinite contrivance is a simple act of will.

What I have just said sounded like explanation, but when I think further about it, I see that nothing has been explained. I still do not know why any single sparrow meets an untimely end, nor why (for it was no deliberate choice) I was moved on this occasion to reprieve a thrush. What I have learned is only that I should be content with what God shows me. In the life of any creature he shows me an actual providence, striking root in an infinite past, and drawing its materials from a universe. Where I have no such clue to follow, I have no such understanding. Where I cannot see providence, I do not see improvidence; I simply do not see. And what sort of religion is it, to stand there complaining at the lack of an impossible knowledge, when I might be adoring a living wisdom everywhere visibly displayed? Is there not enough for contemplation in a sparrow?

God looked on all that he had made, and found it very good, and it is in the light of the achieved goodness that we understand the wisdom which fabricated it. When I see the thrush, quick to recover, shaking his brown silk feathers into place and bustling away, I do not ask whether it is good that such a creature should be; I am made in God's image and God's own praise of his creation finds an immediate echo in my mind. And as I acknowledge the good of the thrush's being, I am furnished with a clue to the providence which has brought it about.

It is more necessary that I should acknowledge the providence of God in human life than in any bird's. God's way with sparrows may mark out a path for my meditation; only his way with me

can direct the steps of my obedience. How am I placed for understanding his dealings with mankind?

So far as the natural goods of our life are concerned, it is
with men much as it is with sparrows. A beautiful and gifted
person, like a pretty sparrow, has been collected from the four
corners of the universe and shaped by an infinity of circumstances. Like the bird, he may be killed or maimed or spoilt, and
will not in any case outlive a measurable time. But beside natural
goods which perish, God has prepared for man a supernatural
good everlastingly to endure, and a providence excluding accident
attaches to this good alone. 'Who shall separate us from the love
of Christ? Shall tribulation or anguish or persecution or famine
or nakedness or peril or sword? Even as it is written, *For thy
sake we are killed all the day long; we have been accounted as
sheep for the slaughter.* Nay, in all these things we are more than
conquerors through him that loved us. For I am persuaded that
neither death nor life nor angels nor principalities nor things
present nor things to come nor height nor depth nor any other
creature shall be able to separate us from the love of God, which
is in Jesus Christ our Lord.'

The workings of this supernatural providence are to be understood by reference to their goal. By looking at the universe I
could never have divined that it was working towards a sparrow
or a thrush, until such creatures actually appeared; and by looking
at the whole·confusion of the human scene I could not see the
life of the World to Come prefigured in it. The thrush is before
my eyes, for God has finished that work of his, and shown me
that it is good; and to trace it back to its origins is a task for
science. Napoleon and Socrates are before my mind; psychology
and history may explore what lies behind them on the natural
plane. But our future glory is not the object either of sight or of
thought; we know not yet what we shall be; we cannot stand on
the pinnacle of that mountain where all the saints were manifested
to S. John in company with the Lamb, his name and his Father's
name written on their foreheads, their ears filled with floods and
thunders of angelic singing. Viewed from that height the sides of

the mountain will be seen veined with converging paths, all the ways eternal providence has led the saints to their united goal. But to us below, casting about for the path of our ascent on the flanks of the hill, there is no such simple clarity about the ways of God.

But though we 'know not yet what we shall be,' we are not left without a clue. For 'already we are the sons of God' and 'we know that we shall be like him.' The likeness has been manifested in Jesus, and his face has been multiplied in the saints. Thus it is the formation of Jesus among men, and that alone, which marks out for us on earth the direction of supernatural providence. That grace of God which 'works all things together for good to those that love him' is, says S. Paul, a grace which has 'fore-ordained them to conformity with the image of his Son, that he might be the firstborn among many brethren,' and that the name 'Son of the Father,' branded on the head of the Lamb, might mark the foreheads of the flock.

An unexpected violence of encounter showed me the thrush, though thrushes are everywhere, and I see them, yet have no eyes for them. And Jesus is everywhere, looking out from so many eyes; but it is rarely that the scales fall from mine and I look straight back into them. So I may talk of providence, but cannot trace it, because I do not see that life which the hand of providence feeds. Anything may scatter my blindness, very likely the bird in the net, another's spiritual trouble; or it may just as well be my own. Where the mesh cuts, we begin to take notice of the wings.

It would be a great error to suppose that the providence which works our eternal good concerns itself with spiritual events only, leaving the physical world to be ruled by an indifferent fate. No, the Father in whom we believe is almighty, that is, he has an entire mastery of all things; and we are told that he works all things together for good to those that love him, not spiritual things alone. If the tribes of Israel had perished in the Red Sea and the Wilderness, if Sennacherib's rams had been better handled against the walls of Jerusalem, or hygiene studied better in his camp, if Blessed Mary had lacked physical ability to bear and suckle a child, then the whole manner in which our salvation was brought about would have been different. Indeed, we can have no idea on such suppositions how it would have been brought about. But all these things were under the hand of God's providence. The people of God survived their dangers; Mary conceived a son at Gabriel's salutation and bore him in a stable.

The saints of Israel knew they were governed by a peculiar providence, and received some stirrings of inspiration towards an understanding of it. But it is only in looking back from the achieved result, Jesus Christ, that we comprehend what that providence was. We, like the men of the Old Covenant, look forward to a future good. And though the direction of that good is marked out for us, as it was not for them, since we have seen the Lord's Christ, yet we do not know what path will lead us or our friends to it. And so we do not firmly grasp the providential bearings of our physical inheritance, our national allegiance, our worldly circumstances, the masters, friends, or partners in life who have fallen to our lot; nor, in a wider field, the providence which rules the Church in every kind of economic or political accident. Yet all these things are 'the finger of God,' and not least the seeming disasters which are the extreme proof of saving grace. We are the disciples of a crucified Saviour, and out of his cross and sepulchre came his resurrection.

It is the constant arrogance of my mind, to think that I can make myself and order my existence. My pride is willing to acknowledge that I receive from you, my God, laws of conduct, and a goal, and a general supporting grace; but I acknowledge no more. The rest I think is mine: mine to devise in detail what is good for myself, and for my fellow-men too, in co-operation with them; mine to impose the scheme of wisdom on the passive material of life. But the material proves anything but passive and the plans never succeed; or if they succeed, the success is formal and the fruits are ashes. And so I fret incessantly, and complain of the whole frame of the world which you have made. O God, when shall I consent to be your creature? To make myself, I must re-make the world, for I am inseparable from it; and I cannot make, nor re-make, the world. Certainly I am bound to think and plan and contrive, or I should not be a living man; yet always with submission, always attentive to the pressures and resistances of your fingers, as you mould in us the clay of Adam's kind.

O my folly! The world of my plans, how narrow, and bare, and stale it is! And the world which breaks my plans, how living, and various, and wide, and glorious it is! And from every point in it a providence bears upon me, to make me the man you intend : here a claim, there a discipline, here love to cherish, there enmity to vanquish, and everywhere Christ. Be not anxious, says Christ, not that he may make us careless, but that he may lift our faces out of the book of our calculations and sweep the cobwebs of self-obsession from our eyes. If I gave my attention to your handiwork, I should become your handiwork. Make me open to each thing and person in their turn, that I may not only love them, but be directed through the providences which speak in them.

If I attended to them, and if I were faithful to you! How little right I have to complain that your providence is hidden! How often you have shown me the track of your purpose, and I have walked in it for a few paces, then struck out of it. Do not show me only, seize my hand and drag me, until I come to know and love the path. How can I know your particular counsels, who will not do your whole bidding as it is daily signified to me, but pick and choose? If I followed any track of your commandment faithfully to the end, it would open into another, and so into another, all the way to heaven.

I know the God of mercy by my sins, I cannot know the God of providence except by my obedience. Your mercy and long-suffering have brought me to repentance a thousand times, and shown me the path, but I have not persevered in it. There is no knowledge of your ways except by walking in them. I cannot see, for I walk against the sun. How well I have begun to see, when I have turned down the direct path of your rays!

Lord I believe

I will give thanks unto thee, for I am fearfully and wonderfully
  made : marvellous are thy works, and that my soul knoweth
  right well.
My bones are not hid from thee : though I be made secretly and
  fashioned beneath in the earth.
Thine eye did see my substance, yet being imperfect : and in thy
  book were all my members written,
Which day by day were fashioned : when as yet there was none
  of them.
How dear are thy counsels unto me, O God : O how great is the
  sum of them!
If I tell them, they are more in number than the sand : when I
  wake up, I am present with thee.
Try me, O God, and seek the ground of my heart : prove me
  and examine my thoughts.
Look well if there be any way of wickedness in me : and lead me
  in the way everlasting.

> My God and my All
> My beginning and my end
> My sole and everlasting good
> My God and my All.

CHAPTER IV

I believe in Jesus Christ his only Son who sitteth on the right hand of God the Father and in the communion of saints

I SEE the hill behind the houses and the stars behind the hill, and a science which has more delicate instruments than eyes to judge by, informs me of stars and stars beyond the stars I see. Out of a depth which drowns my sight and starves my imagination they throw their beams to touch and penetrate the back of my visible stars. My living soul assures me that all these have actual being. If I am assured of anything, I am assured of the life which heaves in my breath and tingles in my veins. My feeling soul extends to the boundaries of my body, and there its action ends, but not its exploration. Sense sliding out along the perpendicular lines of light comes up with sun and stars and annexes them to the sphere of vision; and where sight ends, thought builds the base-camps of ascent and scales the invisible sky. Knowledge fans out from the body of a man to the bodies which form the place of his existence, and so out and out to the bodies beyond these, until the universe of stars becomes his place. I am accustomed to plot the position of anything I may conceive, somewhere in the unending field of bodies; and if I should say of a thing that it is beyond the fringes of the field, I should merely extend the field a point further by saying it, and far enough to include the thing of which I speak.

Where, then, in all my spreading world is Jesus Christ, risen and glorified? When the cloud received him out of our sight, into what height, what distance did he go? However far I take him, I gain nothing by it: it is no easier to place him beyond Orion than to place him behind the nearest trees. His risen being is no part of our interlocked system of natural forces, whether far or near. He is nowhere in our world, but neither is he outside it,

33

c

for to place him outside it is only to place him in the fringes of it. Where then is he?

The only way to find Heaven is to begin from Heaven. Jesus in his glorious manhood is the heart of Heaven, as each of us is the heart and centre of our visible world. He is assured of his world as each of us is assured of ours—by the vigour of his existence; and as the acts of his life are more intense and wakeful than ours, he has less reason than the best employed of us, ever to take it for a dream. Even less than ours is his life locked within his breast; radiating through lines of heavenly interchange his soul knows what is next to him, blessed saints whose society is the place of his existence; and on and on, without failure or weakening of sight, his eyes embrace a universe of spirits, as many as the stars we see; without any thinning or flattening of sound he may converse with the distant as with the near, and receive from every one a voice, expressing in unique and personal colour the glory and the love of God.

At first it may seem that we have two universes, spreading on independent planes and nowhere touching at a single point : Christ's universe of spirit, ours of natural forces. Yet, thinking further, we may see that while it is impossible to place Heaven in the world, it is impossible not to place the world in Heaven. If Christ's knowledge is spiritual as ours is physical, he knows us, for we also are spirits, though in fleshly bodies. He knows us, indeed, by that special fellow-feeling of a creature for its kind, which makes hearts tuned in the same scale to sound in unison, for 'he took not on him the angelic kind, he took the seed of Abraham.' If, then, he hears our voices and thinks our thoughts as fast as we can form them, he feels also in our fingers and looks through our eyes; he lives out along the lines of our vision, and our sun, moon and stars are his. By sympathy Heaven grafts the world into itself, and roots our universe in its own heart.

Jesus Christ, then, lives in the same world with us, and we in the same Heaven with him, and it is in what passes between him and us that our salvation lies. It is not merely that he exists, and I exist. We coexist, and coexistence implies mutual influence. Even in the physical world it is impossible for two things to coexist, though at the extreme opposite limits of the universe, without affecting each other. Everything plays a part in the environment of anything. What does nothing to us is clean out of our world; it provides us with no clue for suspecting its existence. The world of persons, even as commonsense acknowledges it, offers an analogy. That strange corporate force, the Western European mind, so alarming and so baffling to the Russians, is a resultant of individuals in multitude, and every one of us, in however minute proportion, goes to colour or intensify or dilute it. And when we come to smaller personal worlds where each one counts for more, who is to estimate what we do to one another by coexisting? How, by being what we are, and without the least intention, we infect and heal, encourage and depress, poison and purify the people about us, and receive from them a reciprocal influence?

Balaam, the old magician in the Book of Numbers, was credited with such a power that those whom he blessed were blessed, and those whom he cursed were cursed. Hemmed in and threatened by the God of Israel, he got a wholesome fear of uttering spells outside the direct line of God's revealed will. What frightens me is not the magic which I may be tempted, like Balaam, wilfully to utter, but what flows from me unheeded and is beyond my power to shut off. God forbids me, as he forbade Balaam, to curse whom he has not cursed, or to defy whom he has not defied. But the defiance and the cursing issue from me without a word said, and darken the air. If God is to be obeyed in this, he must bestow what he demands, he must make in me a pure and loving heart.

Heaven lives by its own laws; we have to live by the laws of earth and by the laws of Heaven too, and, in particular, so to act within the prescriptions of earthly law, that the laws of Heaven may take effect. In Heaven mind touches mind and love touches love, and by such contact the blessed know one another. On earth also these touches take place, but largely unperceived by both parties. When Jesus knew that the woman had been healed by the border of his garment, it was felt by those present as a miracle, in which the laws of Heaven rather than of earth had taken effect; for Jesus had not been touched—fingers on a hem swinging loose make no impress on the wearer's body. It was Christ's spirit which felt the touch of faith. What happened in the woman was mixed, part earth and part Heaven. It was heavenly that her faith should lay hold of divine virtue, it was earthly to lay hold of it in a physical sign, the border of a garment.

On earth the touch of love with love, or of hatred with dislike, or of any meaning or intention in the mind with another mind, is expressed in conduct, conveyed through speech, steered and directed by gestures of the hands, or hinted in the corners of the eyes. But if we live with those we love, the proportion of meaning divined to sign exhibited becomes so great, that we cannot suppose the means of communication to do more than suggest or guide a deeper and closer touch of mind on mind. And so we do not start with surprise, but rejoice in a familiar secret, when we one day read the thought of our friends out of motionless silence and with no signs given at all : or when, being separated from us, they write to us and tell us our thoughts and cares which they have suddenly divined; or merely take up their pens to write after a long interval in the same moment as we take up ours—the letters cross, and we quarrel for the honour of having remembered first, and moved the ether which moved the other to write. The dying soldier shouts on the field of battle, or the sailor drowning at sea, and his wife or mother hears him in her bed. And those who will not believe history unless they can create it under controlled conditions arrange experiments in telepathy and clairvoyance which, however trivial in substance, add something to proof.

The meaning passes from mind to mind, but we cannot make it do so except by giving signs. The sense outruns the words, but we cannot assure the transmission of what we do not express. We must act by the laws of earth, however much we hope the laws of Heaven may take effect. Yet who am I that I should invoke the laws of Heaven to extend my action, full as I am of a poison and a mischief I cannot control? And what is it that I ask Heaven more inwardly to impress on my neighbour's mind? The meaning I contrive to stamp with the superficial decency of word and gesture, or the unacknowledged disposition of my heart? Midas who asked that all he touched should turn to gold bitterly regretted the obtaining of his request, and if the walls of my heart were made glass in answer to my prayer, the hurt to my neighbour's eyes and the shame to my conscience would be equal.

As it is, my spiritual disease disquiets my neighbours, but by the mercy of God they do not for the most part know the source of the disturbance, or even that they are being disturbed. I contribute my mite to the sum of sadness, the impersonal mist by which we darken one another, and which we take to be the air of the world. My words and deeds, my neglects and interferences are enough to answer for, and I shall read the scroll of them on the Day of Judgment. But even when I see myself in the pupils of the eyes of God, shall I be made aware of all the poison that has flowed from me, not by what I did, but by what I was? Will even the rigour of the last account exact so much?

Let me then, like the woman in her impurity, reach for the hem of Christ's garment, that I may touch heavenly virtue, and the river of death which runs from me may be stayed. What our dress conceals, his dress shall banish, the defilement which hidden from the eyes infects the air. Christ is in the world with me, and I am in Heaven with him. His action is heavenly and needs no earthly means, he touches me by spirit and by love, and who can tell how he affects me, unknown to myself? Yet I must turn and touch him, too; and my action must be earthly, for it is only by earthly actions that I can direct my affections. I must form words to speak to him, I must eat his body in the bread he has given, and drink his blood in wine. I must so act within the prescriptions of earthly law, that heavenly law may take effect.

God has saved us by sending his Son into the world that we may live through him. It is not that, apart from Christ, we are cut off from the fountain of living waters, it is that no other can cure us of poisoning the spring. There is no source of life but one, God, and nothing lives that is not fed continually by his creative act. Where secular wisdom sees a single fact, the action of our personal life, faith sees a double fact, the soul in God and God in the soul. The analyses of psychology do not draw the line between the two. They may divide my image of God from my image of myself, but my image of myself is not myself, neither is my image of God the person of God. In the formation of both images, and in the play of my various affections round them whether by way of attraction or repulsion, both God and the created soul are at work, God acting through the soul, and the soul by derivation from God.

In a holy action the division between the divine source and the human stream cannot be felt, for then God's will for his creature and what the creature does are simply the same; the creature is most himself by expressing God. In an unholy action the division cannot be felt either; for unholiness is a living lie, the self-stultification of the creature's spirit, an active will not to know the fountain of our origin. How sin resists and alters omnipotence is a mystery which can never be understood. It could only be understood in the act of sinning, if sin could understand itself. And sin neither can nor deserves to understand itself; sin is the voluntary self-confusion and self-darkening of the intellect on the side which faces God. God and our relation with God can only be known when our life is a self-drawing out of the fountain of life.

What have I to do, then, but to put myself back into God and to live out of God? But how am I to do this? The general intention is not enough; the wish to be rooted in God is like the wish to be happy. It is not enough to wish, I must know the road to take and the road must be under my feet. It is not enough to throw myself back into whatever the name of God may turn out to stand for, or I shall be throwing myself in no direction rather than another. And if I throw myself into what I take to be God, it must be God in so far as his likeness is expressed in my mind, and that will be a distortion, if I am a sinner. But why should I depend upon my thoughts of God, since we are all members one of another, and other men's thoughts have as much prestige with me as my own? Indeed, what I take to be my own thoughts are in all likelihood not mine, but passed a hundred times from hand to hand, and now so accepted by me, so grown into the stuff of my mind, that they are all the me there is. What, then, is the authority of these common thoughts? What are they but the remorseful aspirations of a sinful race?

We are all members one of another, and one of us is Jesus Christ, God and Man. He is the Son of God, and his Sonship is simple and unalloyed derivation. We wind up our buckets half empty and spilling as they come out of the well of life; in him the fountain rises to the surface and overflows. It is his glory to be derivative. He seeks not his own praise, but the praise of his Father, the works he does are not his own, but his Father's works, nor is it he that does them, but his Father in him. If the words we write are derived from a model, our work may be decried as derivative. But no one will complain of the derivativeness of the writing, if the source from which it derives is the author's mind, for that is the derivation which guarantees the life and spontaneity of the work. The Son of God is the Word of the Father, and more alive than any utterance, because he comes new every moment out of the heart of God. And he is with us in the world, and we in Heaven with him. His life touches ours, we reach out our hands and touch his garment's hem. We pray our prayers through Jesus Christ our Lord, aspiring to pray in one piece with him, in one mystical body, because with him is the well of life, and in his light we see light.

When I touch Jesus Christ, I touch him who touches all; when his virtue comes into me, there runs in me that which clears all eyes and enlivens all hearts. While my hand supports and caresses my own head my feeling is a circuit returned upon itself, but when I stretch out my hand and touch Christ, the circuit of affection runs through all creatures, and especially through those who love him. When I see men by themselves every one is a distinct and separate force, bearing on my own action in one way or another, whether welcome or unwelcome; when I see men in one world with Christ, everyone is a soul on whom Christ bears as he bears on me, and in whom some impress of his virtue may be seen; everyone has alive in him, recognized or unrecognized, a brotherhood with Christ endeavouring to be itself.

Father Almighty, Maker of heaven and earth, what shall we give you, what have we that you desire? You desire our love and you desire to do us good, and these two desires are one. For if we turn to you in love we shall receive you into ourselves, and if we admit you into ourselves you will do us all the good you have prepared for us. You desire that we should put back into your hands all that your love has made us, in longing after all that your love will make of us, and in adoration of all that your love is. I can say the words, I cannot do the thing : I am not the master of my heart. What I give I give with part of my mind, and what I give now I shall take back in half an hour. My rooted longing is after vanity and pleasure; I love your love little, my mind being mostly turned from it. Father Almighty, look upon and receive the only acceptable offering, the love of your beloved Son. Regard this prayer of ours not as it is in us, but as it is in him, who prays it in hope ahead of us, and in sympathy along with us. In us it is an episode, a patch of gold cloth on a threadbare garment; in him it is all of one piece with his life and his death, it is that part of his heart which embraces us. This prayer, even in our praying it, shall not be ours; we will go into the heart of Jesus Christ. We will dare, as well as we can do, to be your blessed Son, praying for your Name to be hallowed, your kingdom to come, your will to be done. We will explore the cares of his heart for his Church, and for our friends, and for our perfection.

When I pray it is a double acknowledgment that I cannot save myself; for first, if I could save myself, why should I pray? And second, I cannot of myself direct my prayer; I must have recourse to Jesus and take direction from his. But even so, I cannot save myself, not even by adhering to Jesus in my prayer;

for I cannot always pray, nor so much as recollect. I go about my business or my pleasure and leave the care of myself to Christ; his invisible and unremembered love which suffered for me before I was born and first brought me to speak a word of prayer, must bring me back to my knees, or I may never pray again; and so keep me in my way, that I may arrive still a Christian at the place of prayer. He will not disappoint us, we shall be everywhere surrounded by him as by the atmosphere. Heaven is full of his saints, and earth of the men out of whose eyes he looks upon us. Moreover he is enthroned, though disregarded, in the heart. He will not leave us empty.

Let me recall our common Christian knowledge, let me repeat the speech of Love himself.

'I brought you into being that I might love you, and what shall I so love in you as your love? Do not tell me that it is small. Is my mind like yours, to consider one thing at a time and to let the small be crowded by the great? Have I not more than all the love for which any of my creatures provide the mark? You can-not set me up a target so quickly as I will fill it with the arrows of my fire. My eyes go through you, and you think they find nothing; but I see the abyss beneath the shallows. I follow the root of your will through the sand of vanity to where it is fixed in the heart of my Son. He says you are his, he owns you for part of himself, he bears your sickness and counterworks your evil. You express to me that dear Person in whom I am well pleased.'

My God, I love you because you are good above all others; and I love my neighbour for your sake.

CHAPTER V

I believe in Jesus Christ who was conceived by the Holy Ghost and born of the Virgin Mary and suffered under Pilate

THOSE who play with homing-pigeons send them away in baskets to various places previously determined, and there they are let go. They wheel about the sky so many times that we tire of watching them, and as though they were casting about for a track or a scent lying in the air. Then, just as we drop our eyes, they are suddenly gone, flying straight to their invisible mark. So God deals with his spiritual creatures. By the dark secret of creation he expels them in various directions and to various depths of space. By their births they are released, and in their lives wheel round their native sky, feeling for the invisible attraction of the Creator's spirit, by which he will guide them to himself. And so they fly in to him by those various paths and approaches of love which distinguish them in his eyes from one another. Here the parable fails, for the pigeons arrive and rest on the perch; whereas the spiritual creatures rest on the wing, upheld by the God who draws them ever more deeply into the infinite heart of light.

There are two places which determine the path of any soul, the place of its creation from which it takes wing, and the place of its destination to which it flies. If we think of any saint now in his blessedness, we must think simply of the man he was, and of the God into whom he continually goes; out of those two we must be content to compound his present being. The womb was his cage, his birth was the fixed moment of his release; and yet his creation was not then completed; while he explored the sky and picked up the direction of his course he was being made himself, and distinguished by his acts or sufferings from all other creatures. And whether that making, that distinguishing and individuating, ever ends, who can tell? Who knows whether there ever comes a time when the existence of the blessed is no longer a making, but simply a drawing into God and a filling with God of that which has been once for all made?

However it may be with the saints, we may say with confidence of Christ, that he was fully made the man he became by his birth, life, death, descent into hell and resurrection; so that his present human being is nothing but the continual return of his manhood to God and fulfilment with God. If we knew two things, the Divine Nature and Christ's history on earth, we should know Christ in heaven. In fact we know little of either, but enough of each to lay hold of Christ and therefore of our salvation. The rest of his history is not the story of how he became himself, but of how he has colonized the hearts of his saints, multiplying himself and building up his empire.

Our life is each of us, and Christ's life is Christ; and more completely so, because in him there was no wavering of purpose, no cause for him to amputate or renounce any part of what he had been. The stream of his life ran in one channel, and flowed steadily towards the goal of his desire. Of no part of it had he need to say 'There I was not myself.' Because he did not falsify, therefore he did not repent.

It is surprising how easily we take for granted what we are. I know my body, if not as a physician knows it, yet practically, and as it concerns me. But how do I know my mind? I am inclined to think of it as a present object of knowledge; but there is little present at this moment to my perception of myself beyond the half-sentence I am now throwing into words, together with the vague confidence—a confidence I should scarcely know how to justify—that thoughts I have not yet conceived will draw my meaning on to some conclusion.

If I lay down my pen and take stock of myself, I may say that I am a man who enjoys such and such pursuits and is wearied by others, a man who has one degree of friendship for this person and another degree for that. Yet the weariness and the enjoyment I impute to myself are nothing actual here and now, for I am not now engaged in the pursuits that occasion either; and in the future I may learn to like what has hitherto disgusted me or come to tire of what I previously enjoyed. I think of my friendships as constant realities, yet they are not taking effect here and now. I simply assume that my former likings, my former aspirations and policies continue to point in the directions in which they pointed when they were last in active employment. My past has set the moulds of what I am : I am all of my past which I have not revoked, and a great part of what I supposed I had revoked. What I shall be to-morrow I do not know, except that neither external circumstance nor inward decision will have had time to alter much of what yesterday has made me. I am my life, or all of it that I have not shaken off. If I had lived a better life I should be a better man, but without a life behind me, bad or good, I should be no man at all.

We say that Christ became man in Mary's womb at Gabriel's salutation; that is, he entered the human sphere then, he became the seed or element of a man. But in the sense in which none of us became a man before he had been a child, he was not a man until he had grown in wisdom and stature. Each of us becomes a man, a person, from being almost nothing, as a line drawn out on paper begins from a point. He, from being all there was to be, became man also; but he too drew the line of his manhood out from the bare point of birth and, indeed, of conception. He took manhood on him to redeem it, and this he did progressively through his whole life, entering at every step more deeply into the manhood he had taken. When he reached maturity and finished the work, he died, and went through hell into heaven, all the needles of his human concerns and loves pointing as his life and death had set them. This is the man Jesus Christ; this is the Christ with whom we have to do. What went further to his being was not the making of his manhood but the fulfilling of it with his Father's presence.

Being innocent of sin, he made all choices wholesomely in his mere infancy, and uprightly when he became the master of his acts. But being born a member of our race, and drawing the stuff of his experience and the furniture of his mind from our corrupted stock, he had constantly to correct the vice of crooked tools and experienced as temptation the bias he resisted. Or let us say that he had entered on the worn channel of our path, and went straight by constantly breaking out of the crooked groove, forcing his way in the line of greatest resistance.

The story of Christ's temptations in the wilderness is obstinately interpreted by Christian reverence as the description of very subtle and refined suggestions about the mismanagement of his unique vocation. The reverence is misplaced and the interpretation mistaken. The Evangelists' intention is exactly opposite: they press Christ's temptations into the common mould of Israel's, as typically experienced by the people in the wilderness, or as applied by the rabbinic preacher to the ordinary dangers of his hearers. Certainly the temptations of Israel are not the temptations of man in his natural life, but of man called into divine sonship. Instead of making their requests known to God in a spirit of faith, his children complain of their wages, and clamour for their needs to be supplied in a way of their own choosing; they 'murmur for bread.' It is but a step more and they are found to be 'tempting God,' that is, putting him to the test, forcing his hand to work them miracles if he is not to lose them. The last step is apostasy, a door into the direct possession of a world which triumphant heathenism has in its gift.

Christ's temptations, say the Evangelists, were of the common pattern, however weighted with the burden cast on obedience by the highest, and on faith by the most mysterious, of all vocations; complicated, too, by the awareness of intrinsic royalty and more than natural powers. He was tempted at all points as we are. As his day, so was his strength; but as his strength, so was the burden of his day. His temptations were as great as his task and his task was as great as himself. If his godhead bestowed unique grace on his human will, it was not to make easy for him what for us is difficult, but to make possible for him what we could not begin to attempt.

He made himself, he built his human greatness stone by stone,

Lord I believe

choosing love daily and rejecting evil. Every such choice renewed and affirmed his union with his Father's life. By every act he committed himself wholly, so far as any man can commit himself by any act. But our human condition does not allow us to prefabricate our moral future. To-day's acts make us what to-morrow will find us, and yet, being what we are to-morrow, we shall have to remake ourselves then by fresh decisions. The situations will be new, the temptations new. Though every act of Christ's was perfect, none of them was final except the last, nothing irrevocable but voluntary death; his manhood was not nailed to what it was, until the hammers of his executioners had done their work. Taking the road towards Jerusalem he three times prophesied his passion to his disciples; by his righteous acts in the Temple he drew upon himself the powers which would kill him; he gave himself away with his own hands at the supper table. Yet in Gethsemane he sweated blood over the acceptance of his bitter cup, as though that were the first occasion of its confronting him.

Moral consistency, if we could attain it, would not lie in the power to mortgage our future freedom, but in the ability to reaffirm our past by every fresh decision; and such was the integrity of Christ. He did not, like the obstinate and impenitent, reaffirm the policy of his previous acts because they had been his; he continued steadily in his Father's love, and found himself abiding by what he had always been.

We make a difficulty to ourselves over Christ's temptations because (we say) no temptation can be real unless there is a possibility of our falling to it. But since Christ was the Son of God, he was not going to fall in any case. The essential point here is that we should see in what the impossibility of his sinning lay. If it lay in the virtual fixing of his choices before he made them, then indeed he had no temptations, nor was his life a human life at all. But suppose it lay in a perfect trust reposed by him in his Father, assuring him that in all the unseen possibilities and sudden temptations of the coming time, his Father's power and Spirit would not fail him? On the occasions when we faithfully invoke and lovingly receive it, the assistance of God does not remove the reality of our decisions; when we are most in God, then we are most freely ourselves. And if we persevered in an entire and unbroken dependence, we should cease to sin, but we should neither cease to be tempted nor to make hard decisions.

Such, then, was the life of Christ. Certainly there was something fixed and inflexible about him, but it was not a pattern of moral choice forestalling all surprises, it was divine Sonship, filial love, absolute dependence, entire derivation. That completion of Christ's manhood by his death, and fixing of it in a love which can never be revoked, was a grace for which he trusted his Father, and which he earned by frequent prayer; so that almost the last breath of his expiring life was heard to shape the appeal of the psalmist's deep distress, My God, my God, why hast thou forsaken me?

The mystery of Christ's saving death is endlessly explored and never exhausted; but nothing about it, surely, is plainer than this, that it was death as it ought to be died. Death seals and determines the achievement of life, surrendering it into God's hands, to be changed and used for new purposes. But where the ends of life have not been truly attained, death seals and perpetuates frustration. If in our life we have entangled ourselves with vanity, death fixes us in the entanglement and there leaves us, unless an unmerited mercy will deliver us. Even if we are so to be delivered, our death itself has not been salutary, but disastrous; has not freed us, but knotted the bonds which mercy must untie. The death of Christ is a dying into life, the death of sinners a dying into death. Lazarus is bound hand and foot with his graveclothes and blindfolded by the headcloth, until Christ sets him free. Christ cannot be bound, but goes his way, leaving the clothes folded.

It is not the hour of my death, but the fixity of my death that matters. I may live until I am weary of life and able to do nothing but faintly fret at the fixity of frustration into which I have virtually died already. We may die by inches; the day to be feared is not the day of our dissolution but the day of our fixation.

Nature will always, when she feels it, abhor bodily death; but this natural abhorrence need not be always present to the mind, and faith could often look cheerfully at death if she could know that the golden hours entrusted to her had not slipped through her fingers, but had been expended heedfully on the pearl of great price. If I could see the purchase of my spending in the happiness of my friends or in familiarity with God's love, I might not grieve to die, nor wish to have the spending of my time again.

What I have just said would belong in the mouth of a man who looked for resurrection, but not through Christ. A Christian is a man baptized into Christ's death, united with the act of perfect sacrifice which is the open road into immortal life. None of us lives to himself, none dies to himself. Our acts of virtue, worthless in themselves, become something as parts of Christ's action, when he who inspires them adopts them and uses them. Our death takes its quality not from the current of will which has become the set flow of our life, but from the current of Christ's love running in us. He who has been willing to adopt our life will not disown our death, nor refuse us the purgatorial discipline which will finally integrate us with his blessed will.

Whatever our future hopes, our present concern is to live ourselves into the living Christ, the man whom God the Son has become by life and death, and whom his Father has crowned with glory and drawn into the society of his love. There are two parts to our consideration of him : there is the man who offers himself to the Father, and there is the Father's acceptance of the man. He offers himself in his passion, he is accepted in his glorification. The movement of his human love continues in the direction which his passion set for it; his glorification continues in the ever new outpouring of his Father's love.

Thus the eucharistic sacrifice, always offered and always accepted, conveys to us the present being of Christ; not a history of two thousand years ago, but the act by which he now exists. The revelation of Christ's enduring love is to be found in the act which gave it its unalterable direction. To speak of Christ's love in his heavenly being alone is merely by an accumulation of superlatives to express the breakdown of expression; the quality of his love is tasted and the substance apprehended in the earthly history of his passion. By bringing down our thoughts to earth, the sacrament sets them in the heart of heaven.

Whether we say that the Eucharist unites us with Christ or with the accepted sacrifice of Christ, makes no difference. Christ is his accepted sacrifice, that is his present being. Taken into his sacrifice we are ourselves both sacrificed and accepted, for we are brought into Christ.

Why was it ever suggested that participation in Christ through the Sacrament is a substitute for participation in Christ through faith? It might as well be said that Christ's dying for us was a substitute for our believing in him. In what do we put our faith? In Christ, and Christ is his life or his action. Christ is the Son of God, born as man, teaching, loving, suffering, dying, and giving the body and blood of his sacrifice to his disciples in bread and wine. There is no other Christ for us to believe in, and we trust him to save us by the acts in which we believe. Christ and his acts are explored and apprehended by faith; faith will consider also how he takes us into his death and resurrection by the sacraments.

We cannot receive the sacraments without faith; yet the grasp of faith on what the sacraments effect need not be at its liveliest when the sacraments are received, but rather, perhaps, in an hour of meditation, perhaps in conversation, perhaps in doing the will of God. On such occasions faith may be granted her strongest apprehension of incorporation with Christ; it may be then that we make free with Christ, and Christ with us, giving us away to his friends.

We celebrate the sacrament with whatever force of faith, whatever charitable intention we can muster at the time. When we leave the altar we do not cease to put faith in the Christ of the sacrament, but continue in our prayers to ask for our smouldering sacramental faith to be blown into a flame. All prayer and all obedience is one with the Eucharist, for it is a participation in Christ's dying love. Our self-giving would not be in Christ, nor real in itself, if we could never recollect and say 'Ah, but he died.'

49

D

Lord I believe

Soul of Christ hallow me
Body of Christ save me
Blood of Christ inflame me
Water from Christ's side wash me
Passion of Christ strengthen me

O good Jesus hear me
Within thy wounds hide me
Suffer me not to part from thee
From the malicious enemy defend me

In the hour of my death call me
And bid me come to thee
That with thy saints I may praise thee
   for ages everlasting.

CHAPTER VI

I believe in Jesus Christ our Lord who was crucified

THERE is a grim humour in the old practice of gamekeepers, to nail up dead stoats and magpies above the pheasant-coop, warning off by their example the rest of their kind. The Roman police did better; they nailed up human enemies, and nailed them up alive. They would still be good propaganda when they were dead and cold, but the cream of the demonstration was the twelve or so hours during which, with luck, they might live in agony on the cross, so that men might point at them, and say, 'Look, this is—not this was, but this is—the disturber of our peace; this is the enemy of mankind. Curse him—he cannot hurt you; throw filth at him—he cannot shoot back; and praise our lord the Emperor, who tramples all our enemies under his feet; thank the army, which gives us everlasting peace.'

So there Jesus hangs—Jesus, the enemy of mankind; Jesus, the ruin of our quiet. We shall not hear that frightening voice any more : that voice more destructive than armed force. To get him hanged, they said he had threatened to pull down the Temple. But that was just to get him hanged. He did not go about things that way. If he had really pulled the Temple down, we would soon have had it up again; but if we had listened to that voice much longer, and felt those eyes upon us, our confidence would have broken beyond repair. The Temple would have been nothing —the whole world we believed in came crashing round our ears while he spoke. We believed in this country of ours—call it Judæa, call it England—as the centre of a spiritual civilization; he talked it into a dry husk, which the wind would presently carry away. We believed in the Great Power over sea to the west, our protector, whose eagles fly over our heads; he told us that the fashion of our world would pass, and all this power would fail us. We believed in ourselves, in our comfortable virtues, our material aims; but hearing him—and what was worse, seeing him, and knowing the man that he was—we felt our self-respect, our faith in ourselves, crumble. He said in so many words that we must perish, to become the men he meant us to be. If any man would go my way, he said, let him renounce himself, shoulder his cross, and come with me to die.

Was this world of ours to end, or was Jesus to be stopped? Who could hesitate for a moment? It is expedient that one man should die for the people, and that the whole nation perish not. So said the High Priest, and how right he was! Which of us does not side with him? Jesus is our enemy. He hurts like conscience, but beyond our power to heal. Conscience tells us the faults we have learnt to recognize; Jesus lets in on our neglected corners the insupportable light of heaven. Conscience tells us to live more carefully our safe, reassuring, worldly life; Jesus opens up those chilly horizons beyond our death, when we shall be stripped of achievements, hobbies, comforts, and possessions, and left with nothing to live upon, but love of God and man. Perhaps it was not clever, after all, to put Jesus on the cross. We wanted to silence his warnings about death; we have put him up to die in front of our faces, and it makes us think that we shall die soon. Better turn our heads away, and go back to the glow of our firesides; where we can put food into our mouths and entertainment before our eyes, and fill our lungs with life. Jesus is the voice of death; let us stop our ears; death is the one enemy we cannot meet.

If Jesus could answer, but his throat is dry and stiff; all the voice he has is scarcely enough for seven short words. If he could answer—but does he need to answer with his tongue? Surely his hanging on the cross speaks louder than any voice; and though no sound is in our ears, our heart can listen.

'Am I your enemy? You are not mine. I have no enemies; I prayed for those who pierced my hands. Look in my eyes. By looking aside you fall into fancies. How easy it is to hate and fear the eyes into which you do not look; how few enemies you have, if you look into their eyes! What do you read in mine? Am not I your friend? And the only friend who can do you lasting good. Ah, yes, fellow-sufferer; to-day you shall be with me in Paradise.

'I am your Creator. I love you, because you are my handiwork. I loved you so much, that when I had made you, I would not let you go; I joined you to my heart by lines of invisible power, so that my spirit should feed your mind. I made you to draw your life from me as the branch draws its sap from the stem. You have cut yourself off, you have set up as your own god. Am I your enemy, because I warned you? Separated from me, you wither and die. Should I have been kinder, not to have told you? I kill your pride; but then, I save your soul.

'The proud men have hung me up, still breathing, between the earth and sky. This is their cunning, their art of propaganda, to nail up a living placard, the enemy of mankind. But I have my cunning, to use their cunning, and let them nail up the Almighty Love. From this high vantage point, let me see if I can make any friends. Is it nothing to you, all you that pass by?'

Christ redeemed us from the curse, having been made a curse for us: as it is written: cursed is every one that hangeth upon a tree.

Speaking of someone's opposition to our schemes, we say light-heartedly: 'I'll soon fix him, never you worry.' Jesus had been a trouble to the priests, but now Pilate had fixed him for them, so they did not need to worry. He could not stir a finger to trouble them any more. If he moved an inch it was an agony. This was the sting of crucifixion, that you had them fixed. You nailed your man to the beam like an old deal plank, and there you had him. That would teach him to meddle with what did not concern him; that would teach him to lift his hand against Cæsar. Let him try to lift it now. He could scarcely move enough to breathe —only just enough—but that 'Just enough' was important. He must be able to expand his chest, in and out, in and out, each time with cruel pain; for once he stopped breathing, his being fixed would have no further interest, he would be dead. But a living man, powerless to move a finger—that, now, was something to gaze at.

They have fixed him, so that he cannot do what he would. But what would he be doing? If those feet were not nailed, where would they go? If those hands were loosed, what would they do? Those feet had walked all the roads of Palestine, bringing everywhere the Gospel of God. It was because all Israel had been visited, that Jesus came at last to Jerusalem, there to finish his work. Those hands had not been sparing of their healing touch; and yet Jesus did not come to heal the body; had he been free, he would not, perhaps, have sought out the sick. Those hands, in a gesture of force, had thrown the market out of the Temple. The mere demonstration was enough; if they had been free, they would not have armed themselves for revolt. These hands, only yesterday—was it yesterday? How long ago it seemed! these hands, these very hands, had given away the body and blood of Jesus to his friends in bread and wine. Now, they might as well stay where they were, nailed to the beam. For a man who has given his body and blood away has no business left in this world, but to die; to die, and make good his bequest.

And so, to have his own way, Jesus needed not to be freed; he had it by hanging there. Heaven knows he would have wished it could have been otherwise, for he wished men would have submitted to the Kingdom of God, gladly and cheerfully, at his first invitation. But since they would not; since there were only two alternatives, to desert his mission, or to press on and die; since this was the way things were, Jesus would rather die. He lost no liberty by being fixed, for in being fixed he had his will.

Of course he had two wills. He had the will of a man, or even, we may say, the will of an animal, the will to live: the horror of death, the detestation of pain. And this will he could not silence for a moment, for it lived in every inch of quivering flesh, it screamed in every tortured nerve. In the garden overnight he had done all a man can do beforehand, to give his will away. He had prayed earnestly, until his sweat ran down : 'If this bitter cup cannot pass me without my drinking it, then, Father, not my will but thine be done.' But no one, not Christ himself, can do his dying beforehand; death cannot be died till it comes, nor agony be borne till it seizes us; and when it came to it, all his animal will cried out against the nails. Yet he had another will, the will which embraced his Father's will, so that his Father's will and his were one : the will of the Son of God; the will to drink his bitter cup to the dregs; not because it was bitter, but because it was our salvation.

Not only those who suffer cruelly, like Christ, but all of us, however soft our circumstances to an outward eye, kick at the destiny to which we are tied, and wriggle on the nails of our easy crucifixion. 'If only I were somewhere else—if I were untied from this difficult marriage—if I were released from this routine—if I could be freed from anxiety—if my health did not cramp my spirits—if only . . . then,' we say, not merely, which is obvious, 'I should be more comfortable,' but, 'then I could begin to do something, instead of merely existing; then, we may even dare to say, 'then I could do something for God.' This is the great deception of the devil, to stop us loving, praying, working, now. It may be God's will you should fight your way out of your misfortunes; it cannot be his will that you should make them a reason to put off living as a child of God.

For the will of the Father stretches from everlasting to everlasting, from before Creation as far as the crown of life in heaven, and there is nowhere a moment that is not carried in the stream of that will, nowhere a point at which he has nothing for us to do, though it be only to wait patiently, or to die faithfully, as Jesus died. No one is free but he who embraces the will of God, and shares in the great energy of love which makes and rules the world. Once we have seen that the will of God, here and now, is our bread and our happiness, what a light, what a liberty, shines on our path.

Jesus was nailed, he could not stir a hand; and yet he had his will; for his will was to do his Father's will, and to save us so. He offered that only perfect sacrifice, he made that whole-hearted self-surrender, which liberates us all. For this is Christian liberty, to have our minds joined with his, and let our whole action and endurance in this world be made part of his offering.

Christ hath said; Lo, I am come to do thy will, O my God. By which will we have been sanctified, through the offering of the body of Jesus Christ once for all.

The soldiers dressed Jesus in a purple robe, they put a sceptre of cane in his hand, and a crown of thorns on his head; they hailed him King of the Jews. The great jest to their minds, the supreme absurdity, was his being what he was. For he was the King of Israel, even though his kingdom was not of this world. When they took him to be crucified, they stripped him of the purple and put his own coat on him. But presently they stripped him of that, too; they hanged him up naked; they stripped him not of royal splendour only, but of human dignity. Only, so far as we are told, they left the wreath of thorns still sticking to his head. Crowned, and naked; the contrast was perfect; and to drive the point home, there hung the royal title on the pole, just over the thorny crown : Jesus of Nazareth, King of the Jews. The King of the Jews, the King of the world, hanged naked up, and reigning from a gallows. That was the jest; and that was the truth—What Jesus meant, and what they meant, could be put into the very same words; the difference was all in the tone of voice. They threw taunts at Jesus which he might have thrown back as boasts. 'Others he saved; himself he cannot save.' No, indeed; he cannot save himself, if he is to save those others : and he would rather save them. That is why we worship him; and that is why his enemies deride him .

Crowns, in that ancient world, stood for two things, victory and kingship. For kingship you had silk or gold, for victory ever-green. The crown of thorns was the parody of a royal crown; yet, being made of twigs, it parodies the wreath of victory, too.

In fact, kings were expected to have both sorts of crown. If a king was to reign, he must at least look like a victorious warrior; kings could not easily survive the admission of defeat. But here was a king whose glory was in the dust; here was a conqueror annihilated. For just look at him. Yes, look at him; view him well; for this is the King who is most royal through being humiliated; this is the victor who conquers through his annihilation. This is the commander who says to his opponents :

'You have won all the battles, but you have lost the war. Surrender to me now. Your ammunition is all spent; I know, for it is all here, sticking in my heart. Your last, your irresistible weapon was to have been my death. You have used it, but you have not stopped me; here I am, still claiming your submission; here I am, still loving your souls. You have hung me here, the picture of a living death; you have not weakened, you have strengthened a thousand times, the pull of your king on the loyalty of your hearts; for see, I die to gain them.

'I came, carrying the flag of peace, of reconciliation with the God who made you. You barred my way with swords and dared me to advance : I came straight on, I stuck upon the points, and here I die on them. You have killed me, but have you killed peace? I leave my flowing blood to plead the cause. This is where love is almighty, and mercy irresistible, when your creator lays down life, to make his enemies his friends.

'You kill me, and you set the seal on my victory. I did not fear to be overthrown by any outside thing, by threat or by force, by insult or by torment. The enemy I had to crush was within : the devil, who has tempted me all my life long, as he tempts you; for I have the same body, the same nerves and senses that you have. I had to go hungry, and my stomach cried for food; I had to labour on, when my limbs cried out for rest; I had to meet resistance, and my heart cried out for affection, my brain hinted compromise. When I had to suffer humiliation, my will was up in arms; when, to meet every temptation, I threw myself upon my Father's aid, the devil told me to be a

man, and stand on my own feet. He whispered to me the cata-
logue of all the things I was missing : Revolt from your obedience, he said, and I will give you all the kingdoms of the earth,
and the glory of them.

'This is the enemy that I have fought : Satan, the maggot
who eats the heart of man. For my Father willed that I should
have your nature, as it was, with all its temptations; and that I
should starve the devil out, by giving him nothing of mine to
feed upon. He willed it, and he has brought it to pass. Take
courage, my friends; I have overcome the world.'

See then that flesh in which the devil lurked, dying inch by
inch on the cross; and once it is dead, the devil has lost. Death
was his last throw, and it was a desperate one. For either it
defeated Christ, or it destroyed the devil. If Christ weakens,
Satan triumphs; if Christ is faithful to the death, Satan loses by
that death whatever foothold he had.

Satan's throw is desperate; so see how he has weighted it.
Mere death is not enough; torment is not enough, though it
is as keen as cruelty can make it. Every pain must be sharpened
by the bitter thought : 'Take this, and this, to show you what we
think of you.' This is his countrymen's assessment of Christ; the
men he loved, the men he came to save say to him through
every pang, 'Death is too good for you, unless you die like this.'

I saw the heavens opened; and behold a white horse;
and he that sat thereon called faithful and true. On his
head are many crowns; and he is arrayed in a garment
sprinkled with blood.

In the late afternoon the soldiers came round to see if the
hanged men were dead. They were to be taken down, out of
respect for the holy sabbath which began at sunset. The two
others who hung on either side of Jesus were alive. They killed
them out of hand by breaking their legs across. Jesus seemed
to be dead, so they saved themselves the trouble; only just to

make sure, one of them jabbed him in the side with a spear. He did not stir, or show the least sign of life. He was dead enough, evidently, and if Joseph the Arimathean wanted to bury him, well, he could.

He was dead; not in the artificially arranged imitation of sleep in which we like to lay out those who have died, but with his eyes staring open, and the pupils set; with his jaw dropped down on his chest. He was dead, and nothing could seem more so. Things naturally lifeless do not strike us with their lifelessness, but the human face from which the spirit has departed is dead indeed. And in no case can this have been more shocking than in the person of Jesus, for we cannot suppose that any face was ever as alive as his had been : alive with kindness and with intelligence. But now he was dead. The bodily machine had broken down and stopped; not suddenly, but gradually, through the long agony, his mind was being broken by his pain, and he was being turned into the lifeless mass which now alone remained, when the soldier jabbed at him with his spear. He was not spared the indignity of going to pieces; death is death.

Death is death; and when we die, we go to pieces bodily; some of us take twenty years over it; Jesus took three hours; but it happened to him, too, since he would not be spared anything that belongs to our common lot. He went to pieces in that human life he had taken; and he trusted, as we all must trust, his Father to take the pieces up, and put them together again. God alone has immortality, dwelling in light unapproachable. At the best we are candidates for immortality, making a claim on our Creator's love; as Jesus himself, during his lifetime, had taught. God had given so much, he said, to Abraham, Isaac and Jacob, that he described himself as their God. The relation is permanent, because God's love is undying : 'I am the God of Abraham, Isaac and Jacob,' he says : 'I am,' not 'I was.' God cannot die, neither will he let them die.

Abraham, Isaac and Jacob are a dream to us; but we see Jesus, dying, and thrown upon his Father's love. God was the God of Abraham, Isaac and Jacob : he was their God, and they were his servants. But God is the Father of our Lord Jesus Christ: he is his Father, and Jesus is his Son. All the time he was in this world, his whole life, his whole action was drawn continually out of his Father's heart; and through being a true Son he came to his early death. What life, what death, ever made such a bid for immortality? If God *has been*, but no longer *is*, the Father of Jesus Christ, then God is not God. But God is God; and he is the Father of Jesus Christ; and Jesus, dying, does not die into death, he dies into life, for he dies away into the hands of his Father; as he himself prayed: 'Father, into thy hands I commend my spirit.'

Jesus makes the bid for immortal life which God's love cannot refuse; but he will not earn this blessing for himself alone; it was not for this that he came into the world. He will not have this blessing, unless he can share it with his friends; and for this reason he gives them in bread and wine his body and his blood: to make them one person with himself, that he may not be raised to immortal life without them. And so he is our Saviour. With a generosity which we shall not understand until we see his face, he extends to us his name, his sonship, his Spirit, his immortality.

Christ Jesus became obedient unto death, even the death of the Cross: wherefore also God highly exalted him.

In thee, O Lord, have I put my trust: let me never be put to confusion, deliver me in thy righteousness.

Bow down thine ear to me: make haste to deliver me.

Draw me out of the net, that they have laid privily for me: for thou art my strength.

Into thy hands I commend my spirit: for thou hast redeemed me, O Lord, thou God of truth.

I have set God always before me: for he is on my right hand, therefore I shall not fall.

Wherefore my heart was glad, and my glory rejoiced: my flesh also shall rest in hope.

For why? thou shalt not leave my soul in hell : neither shalt thou suffer thy Holy One to see corruption.

Thou shalt show me the path of life; in thy presence is the fullness of joy : and at thy right hand there is pleasure for evermore.

CHAPTER VII

I believe in Jesus Christ who died and rose and shall come to judge quick and dead and in the forgiveness of sins

L IGHT is named by contrast with darkness, health with sickness, sanity with madness. In any one of these oppositions, unless I understand the meaning of both the opposites, I can attach no sense to the name of either. If I am to rejoice at the presence of light I must be able to feel the threat of darkness. And so it might seem that a love of good depends on a horror of evil. But the reasoning would be false; for the main pleasure I have in light does not consist in my telling myself that it is light rather than dark, it consists in my being illuminated. 'Now it is light!' however pleasurable a realization, is soon had, and quickly forgotten. But my pleasure in the whole exercise of vision endures. The world of shapes and colours feeds my eyes with inexhaustible variety, and the more I am enjoying the realm of light, the more it absorbs me, and the less leisure it leaves me for telling myself that it is light or that I am in it.

Suppose I were made for the light and had never been out of it; had inhabited a world of pure light—not, that is, a world without shade, but a world without night; had never strained my eyes against the blank of darkness nor felt the privation of the power to see. In such a state, so far from lacking the pleasures of light, I should have them always. True, I should not know the meaning of the word 'light,' as it is used by those who say 'Now it is light' or 'What a blessing the light is!' But that would be no misfortune, always supposing that I were a creature made to swim in light, as fishes are made to swim in water.

In fact, of course, I am no such creature. The pleasure of passing from darkness to light is not, for me, the mere pleasure of escaping from a hideous emptiness; it is the enjoyment of a phase in the rhythm of my nature, and the suggestion of losing so natural a pleasure horrifies me. Though light is the element of wakeful life, dark is the element of sleep, and my happiness is in the alternation. I tire of light itself after fourteen hours, and as I love to sleep, so I love the dark in its season.

So it is with light and darkness, but it is easy to find pairs of opposites which are not thus balanced in the rhythm of my life. I am a creature made for sleeping and waking, I am not a creature made for sanity and madness. Children who grow up sane, and among the sane, enjoy all the pleasures of their sanity in the exercise of a sound understanding. They have the world to explore and to take into their heart. They do not know that they are sane, but that is no misfortune. It is a blessed state to take sanity for granted and to be ignorant of madness. At least, it would be a blessed state, if only there were no madness; and that some men are mad is itself a great evil. Since there are such unfortunates in the world, it is a misfortune, as we grow up, not to discover it. But the misfortune lies in the withholding of our sympathy from others' misery, and not in the lack of a foil to our own happiness. It is a hard heart whose pleasure is increased by the perception of others' evil, and the truth of the condemnation is not altered by the fact that such hardheartedness is, as the Latin poet says, to be found in most of us now or then,

Happy, beside the wave, when tempests roar,
To view another's danger from the shore.

In due course our Christian children grow up and encounter madness, and then we teach them to bless God for the gift of a sound understanding; and in this there is an unalloyed increase of happiness, for it is a happy thing to trace our blessings to their source. This, too, is a part of the enjoyment of our natural condition; for just as it is natural for us to sleep and wake, so it is natural for us to depend on him who neither slumbers nor sleeps. And everything which points our insufficiency sharpens our perception of dependence on our all-sufficing God, and leads us home. So God brings good out of evil and compensates human griefs with divine joys.

It is hard, no doubt, to bless God for a sane mind in the face of another's madness without falling into the sin of the Pharisee, who thanked God that he was not like the publican. But there is no such trial of our virtue when the flaw through which God reminds us of our creaturely condition is in ourselves, and not in our neighbours. It was thus that he dealt with S. Paul. 'Concerning the thorn that pricked me in the flesh,' says the Apostle, 'I thrice besought the Lord that it might depart from me. But now he hath said to me, My grace is sufficient for thee, for power is perfected in weakness. I will most gladly boast, therefore, of my very weakness, that the power of Christ may cover me.' So God uses the evils which shadow our glories not so much to heighten them as to lift us above them, that we may dwell not in them, but in their origin. The encroachments of evil drive good back upon its base, and remind it where its native country lies.

God has no height to reach above himself, his happiness has no home more native that his heart. His goodness has no use for any contrasting ill; he is light, says S. John, and in him no darkness at all, and, says the same Apostle almost in the same breath, God is love. God, knowing all things, knows the possibility of darkness before he has created any caverns for the shade, and the possibility of hateful things before they have arisen. But his happiness does not need such knowledge in order to know itself. It is no part of God's delight in what he knows to reflect that he, at least, has escaped ignorance and error. The divine Father does not congratulate himself on finding nothing in his everlasting Son to hate, nor does he rejoice because his Son loves rather than detests him. He does not (if we may attribute to him the forms of our own thought) ponder how sweet it is to love and not to loathe; he loves, and his joy is in his beloved Son, his delight is in infinite treasures, in having, giving and receiving, in speaking and hearing, in looking and in being looked upon.

God has no sort of use for hateful things, and therefore it is that his hatred of them is absolute. He loves what is lovely in us and above all else, our love. Our refusals of love he hates, and everything that leads to such refusals : our pleasure in unworthy objects, the corruptions, divisions and enfeeblements of our love. His hatred of such things is exactly proportioned to his love for us. He who loves me loves my health, he who loves my health hates my sickness; if his love for me is infinite, his detestation of my evil is immeasurable.

Delight is naturally kindled by delight and God, who loves his children's love, delights in their delighting. How, then, is he disposed towards the causes of unwholesome sadness? The flame of happiness would run and spread, but for the obstacles my words and acts and attitudes oppose to it. How then is God disposed towards these acts and attitudes of mine? Does not he detest them? And what is the fate of things which earn the detestation of almighty love? Is it not that they should be abolished? God's hatred or wrath is, indeed, nothing but this, a simple desire for the abolition of its object; it is not, like mine, a passion. Surely, then, God's will is set to wither the tentacles of my unkindness, when they are twisted round my neighbour's throat.

He strikes at my unkindness, I tell myself, and not at me; he hates the sin, but loves the sinner. Here is a saying which must be true in substance, if there is to be any hope for sinful men; yet it is misleading and dangerous, if it suggests to me that my sin is not myself, but somehow detachable. For this is what Satan most wishes me to believe, and commonly makes me believe. According to Satan, and according to me, my sins occur during moral holidays, when my sober, working self is off the job. If he finds me gullible enough, the devil even tells me that I am not really involved at all, my sin is not the act even of a holiday self; it is a play of moral mice harmlessly tolerated, while I, the lordly cat, pretend to be asleep.

God has bidden me not to let my left hand know it, when my right is extended to the poor. I find the advice bad, and if ever, which is seldom, I put my hand to such a use, I take good care that my whole body should know it well. I spread and

65

propagate the warm tingle of conscious virtue, and make it do for a surprising length of time. When, however, my hand or tongue or brain is busy with mischief, whether against my own integrity or my neighbour's peace, then is the time for Satan and me to follow God's advice and seal the operation off. The seal we use on such occasions is an ingenious contrivance, watertight in one direction, but allowing free passage in the other. It prevents the guilt of the irresponsible organ from contaminating the rectitude of the heart, but it allows the pleasure of the heart free passage into the action of the guilty organ. Although, as Satan and I agree, what so passes the sealed door is not I, yet whatever it is, bathes in mischief, and sets every nerve tingling with the excitement. Is not the deceiver my true friend? How sin would hurt, without him!

I may say that there is always more of me beside the part which sins, and that it is fair to hope the better part will reassume control when I am tired of wicked pleasure. So much is true, but it is a truth which does not palliate my sin, it aggravates it. It tells me that all the time I sin, I am the man who knows better and who need not sin; and yet I sin. Beside my bad desires I have good desires somehow and somewhere alive in my mind; and all Satan's story comes to, when it is robbed of its false colours, is this, that if I abdicate control I shall sometimes, anyhow until I further deteriorate, do good and not evil. I have no intention of being wicked on principle, or doing the worse thing when it is the less attractive. But how much credit will God give me for that? I am the man who abdicates control and embraces self-pleasing veiled by self-deceit, and is there a worse man to be found? God abominates this man, he hates this sinner in his sin. The man he loves is the man he is at work upon, the man he has converted to himself, and will convert again. He loves me in other phases, not in this actual phase. But through this phase he loves the Christ in me, who, though crucified by me, lives in me still.

God's will is set to wither the tentacles of my sin, whether they strangle my own virtue or my neighbour's happiness. But how will he wither them? If he kills me they will wither, but equally they will wither if he makes me alive : if he gives another direction to my desire and turns my lifeblood back into its true channel, these monstrous growths will shrivel and drop away. His detestation will have taken full effect through the victory of his love, his wrath will have found its best instrument in mercy, if he destroys my evil by fostering my good.

God's love arms his anger, for it moves him to hate the enemy of what he befriends; but then his anger lends arms to his love, for it moves him so to befriend his enemies that he starves their enmity. The death of Christ has been called the reconciliation of God's wrath and love; but they need no reconciliation, they are one in God, and the perfect unity between them is expressed in Christ's death. How he hates sin, for he dies to destroy it; and how he loves sinners, for he dies to rid them of it.

The Christ who dies for men makes no comfortable distinction between the sin he hates and the sinners he loves; no, he dies to make them the thing he loves in them. He kills them in his death, to bring them alive in his resurrection. This is the revelation of God's righteousness, that he rejects (and it costs the death of his Son) the lies of the devil. For the devil says that I can remain essentially good, and therefore worthy of my Creator's love, in spite of my sin; and his saying this is the unrighteousness, or crookedness, of the devil. But God says, No, I am a sinner, neither good, nor capable of being loved; but he will love me none the less, for his Son shall die to make me lovable. And his saying this is the honesty, or righteousness, of God. 'For this cause the Son of God was manifested, that he might destroy the works of the devil.'

The collision between sin and love is mortal, but love desires that it should be mortal to himself alone. The drunken driver, headed for the fallen rocks, disregards the signal of danger and when the watchman steps into the road, drives over him and kills him. Then, sobered by the spectacle of death, he stops, and not only saves himself, but understands the cost of his

67

salvation. But the story need not have this ending. The driver, having killed the signalman, may increase his pace, as hoping to escape the knowledge of what he has done. Then presently he meets the obstacle less yielding than flesh, and so is stopped by his own destruction, not another's.

If dying love wakens in us, though slowly, an answering love, turning us from sin, then God's wrath achieves its end through the victory of his mercy. But if not, then in the last resort the tables are turned, and God's mercy takes effect through his wrath. His mercy to his whole creation and his love for its perfection must take effect in the banishment of irreconcilable enemies to an outer darkness having no common boundary with the world of light.

We have met God, and we have God to meet. We have met him, and we have crucified him, we crucify him still. He suffers willingly, so long as our sin is mortified by his death. When we meet him, and see in his hands the impress of the force with which we have hammered the nails, we shall be in hell; but he will draw our eyes to his, and then we shall be in heaven. For we shall see them warm with welcome, alive with exultation, because his love has triumphed and his patience brought us to his feet. Then we shall share his joy, for under the eyes of Truth himself we shall not have the hypocrisy to grieve at what he is most happy to have done; and looking on his wounds again we shall find them terrible no more.

> Those dear tokens of his passion
> Still his dazzling body bears,
> Cause of endless exultation
> To his ransomed worshippers.
> With what rapture
> Gaze we on those glorious scars.

The wounds of Christ are the cause of deep wailing if they are seen as what our sin has cruelly inflicted, but they are the cause of rapture if they are seen as what his love has triumphantly endured. And it is this that prevails with us when we look at him : at him, in whom our salvation lies, and not in us. When we recall what he has done for us already in turning us to repentance and giving us himself, we will not doubt that he will complete until the day of his appearing the good work which he has begun in us.

But in the meantime, why do I do the thing God hates, and why do I believe the devil's lies? It is not even as though the lies were new. A habitual cheat, a thousand times caught out in the same offence, he repeats the stale strategy of fraud and I believe him. He does not trouble to vary the tale, so confident he is in my desire to be deceived, to be cheated into cheating the God who loves me. The rays of God's love and his displeasure fall so clear and direct on my every action, how can I be blind to the truth, even though I wish to be blind? How can I? A useless question; there is no reason for perversity, or it would not be perverse. Nor may I say that perversity is the reason; I am the reason, and in being such a reason I am perverse. I know what God loves, and I neglect it; I know what he hates, and I embrace it, and there is no excuse. But he has died to make me otherwise, and he is patient.

Have mercy upon me, O God, after thy great goodness : according to the multitude of thy mercies do away mine offences.

Wash me throughly from my wickedness : and cleanse me from my sin.

For I acknowledge my faults : and my sin is ever before me.

Against thee only have I sinned : and done this evil in thy sight

That thou mightest be justified in thy saying : and clear when thou art judged.

Lo, thou requirest truth in the inward parts : and shalt make me to understand wisdom secretly.

Thou shalt purge me with hyssop and I shall be clean: thou shalt wash me and I shall be whiter than snow.

Thou shalt make me hear of joy and gladness: that the bones that thou hast broken may rejoice.

Turn thy face from my sins: and put out all my misdeeds.

Make me a clean heart, O God: and renew a right spirit within me.

Cast me not away from thy presence: and take not thy holy Spirit from me.

O give me the comfort of thy help again: and stablish me with thy free Spirit.

Thou shalt open my lips, O Lord: and my mouth shall show thy praise.

For thou desirest no sacrifice, else would I give it thee: but thou delightest not in burnt offerings.

The sacrifice of God is a troubled spirit: a broken and contrite heart, O God, shalt thou not despise.

CHAPTER VIII

I believe in the resurrection of the body and the life everlasting

A FAITHFUL martyr had so fully received his judgment in this life, and had been so taken into the sacrifice of Christ by his death, that nothing any longer stood between him and his crown. He saw it, when his agonies at length were over, high and far off, like a ring of light; and knowing that the mercy of God destined him to wear it, he rose (for nothing held him back) towards it. Now it showed itself to him like the halo which sometimes surrounds the moon on a night of vaporous cloud. The opal colours keep their fixed distance from the moon, making the circle perfect, but there is a ripple in them, undulating with the vapour on which they are painted.

Approaching the luminous crown, he found it to be of great circumference and alive with motion; for it was nothing but a light falling from the glorious person of Jesus on the saints surrounding him. Among the faces which from time to time caught the light some were familiar to him who approached, and he slipped in among his friends, happy to be in such company, but at the same time wondering how he was destined to wear a crown of which he was himself not the ten thousandth part. Feeling the eyes of Jesus to be upon him, he raised his own to meet them. He never saw them, for as soon as the line of vision was joined his soul was rapt away and gone into the heart of Jesus, to see with Jesus's eyes. So looking from the centre he saw the living halo of saints reflect that love which Jesus had for each of them. And so the martyr wore his crown, by union with that head to which all crowns belong.

As his senses steadied and he became somewhat used to his condition, the martyr's perception of his own being and of his place among his neighbours returned. He had a double life:

his own thinking and saying and doing were in fellowship with the saints, and at the circumference; but by identification with the life of Jesus he was at the centre also, reading his heart. For Jesus had no secrets to hide and no treasures to reserve; every door was open.

The martyr found himself in no way confused or perplexed by the double life of his mind. Indeed it had always troubled him on earth that prayer and action required to be practised one at a time. Now at last they had run together and united; he could act at the circumference and rest in the centre. He was at home as he had never been before.

The light which poured from the person of Jesus was the source of light on the faces of the saints, and of the same kind with it, gentle and endurable to human flesh, like the light of the moon. The martyr looked for the sun of that world, the focus of unapproachable fire from which so much reflected brightness was diffused; but he could not find it. His companions told him that he looked in vain. For, they said, the rays of that sun do not act on the eyes of any creature except by reflection in other things. They are everywhere active in creating visible brightness, but they provide no lines up which created vision can run, to see the universal fire behind their origin.

It is not (they said) as though any jealousy withheld the fire from sight. It is not the sort of being that could be seen, except in the power expended on its innumerable effects. To look for it is as though we set out to trace a paradise of streams and fountains to their source, and, diving through the spring, were to find ourselves in an illimitable water, which, being perfectly clear and still, presented no object to the eyes. None of the beautiful variety of cascades and pools would be visibly prefigured in their silent source. To see what the water is able to do, we must dive back through the spring and follow the flow. For though God is a fountain of living water, not passively poured out, but himself devising and directing all that issues from his will; he does not, even so, premeditate his works as we do ours; he does not prepare them in his thought, his thought of them is his creation of them. His making is all in his handiwork, there are no diagrams of it or pictures in his mind which we might explore, if we had access to his thought; only an infinite purity of power which does all things.

To know the thoughts that he thinks towards us (they said) we have only to know ourselves and one another. For this heaven of ours is a state in which all clouding of God's ways by sin or by the opaqueness of an unredeemed body is at an end. His purposes being immediately visible, we have no distinction to make between the divine thought and its effect in us. By listening on earth, however intently, you could not hear the grass grow; but here in heaven by a sort of listening and devout recollection you can hear the creative love speak in the springing of life, and in the inspiration of your own thought as it comes. As the wind on earth spreads waves of shadow through the standing corn, so the love of God stirs the people of the heavenly city, and this is the smile of him who makes the light of his countenance to shine.

The creature goes no further into God than this, but from the other side there is no frontier. Our nature lies open to him who made it, and he has come to inhabit his creation for ever. The Eternal Son displays in Jesus not his creature but himself; he gives himself to be known face to face, eyes to eyes and mouth to mouth. Look back to the centre of the crown, and you have what you seek. Use your eyes, and you see God, use your ears, and hear him; join your voice with his, and speak the words of God to God, adoring the Eternal Father through the Eternal Son.

O my God, 'eye hath not seen, ear hath not heard, neither hath there entered into the heart of man' the provision that you have made for the happiness of your lovers. And yet, as the same scripture declares, you have revealed your bounty to us, for you have given us your Spirit to teach us what you bestow on us. And so by nature these things are not known, and yet by your Spirit they are most surely known; and our state is balanced between this sure knowledge and this blank ignorance. We are utterly ignorant of the conditions of that life: how our hands will be occupied, if we have hands; how we shall perceive, whether through five senses, or fifteen, or one. And since we have no knowledge of these most elementary things and could not understand the truth of them if it were told us, it seems doubly vain to inquire into deeper matters.

Nevertheless it is these deeper matters that you, by your Spirit, have made most certainly known. By what means has your wisdom revealed such a knowledge in the darkness of such an ignorance? You have named to us the elements of our present life, and have told us, not how they will be transformed—for that we should not understand—but how they will be more perfectly reconciled and combined together. When the magnet unites a filing of iron to itself, it unites all the filings to that, and to one another. So you assure us that in drawing and reconciling us to yourself, you will reconcile us with one another, with ourselves, and with the world of your creation.

'The kingdom of the world will become the kingdom of God and of his Christ,' and this will be the first reconciliation. For here on earth our heart is divided between two kingdoms and our mind separated into two camps. We think the thoughts and share the passions, assist the work and receive the benefits of a kingdom in which you are scarcely named by your subjects' lips, much less enthroned by their love; where there is no looking beyond the things that perish, and where deadly sins are accepted customs. And if we try to break out of this world, we break the bond of kindness and are lost to our fellow men. Yet with the better part of our heart we must serve a better kingdom; we must think heavenly thoughts and follow the customs of heaven; we must admit none to be our fellow-citizens who do not acknowledge your Christ.

Out of our double citizenship there arise many betrayals; and those who are truest to both kingdoms are condemned as traitors to the world, and put out of the way of serving it, sometimes by ostracism and sometimes by death. But when you manifest your kingdom over your whole creation, there will be one city and one law and one speech. Then the familiar ways and sayings of the people, and the common motives of their lives, will express the innocent sweet nature implanted by you in a creature not made to live alone. Then the hold of the world upon us will bond us into the very fabric of the heavenly city; then a deep root in the soil of our kind will nourish the flowers and fruits of paradise.

The second reconciliation is of our neighbours and ourselves. This present life assigns us a self which, by the mere law of its physical nature, has an intimate union of purpose with the well-being and success of a single body : a body to which all other bodies are a possible threat, and many of them a necessary prey. And though we have fellow-feeling with our kind, yet in a thousand circumstances of life self-love is an instinct and neighbourliness a duty; instinct acts, and duty limps after to correct it. This misery is not cured on earth, except by the most drastic of remedies. If self is once for all expended on its neighbours in a sacrificial death, then indeed the conflict is ended.

By sense we live inside our skins, by reason we sit on the very steps of your throne and look from that impartial height on ourselves crawling among all that crawl the earth, no more to be regarded than any of them. We must, and yet we cannot, live on both levels at once; we must, and cannot, reconcile sense with reason, appetite with justice, self-love with neighbourly love. Only by an occasional happy visitation do we so care for another that his well-being becomes the sole good for which we have any present appetite, or that his face becomes the companion of our thoughts, covering the accursed looking-glass in which we see the reflection of our own.

But when the Last Judgment strikes the glass from our hands and leaves us nowhere reflected but in the pupils of your eyes, we shall be cured of that partial love and conceive an appetite for what is lovely in itself. Constantly feeding on your perfection, desire will always be satisfied and never assuaged. Discovering you in all things, we shall be specially drawn by what kindred endears to us; loving you the Begetter we shall love what is begotten of you. We shall fall to loving mankind by no effort of virtue, but by simple and single-minded delight.

As for our own being, we shall prize it as the place of happy vision in which you have set us, thence to contemplate you and all your saints; we shall prize it as the instrument with which you equip us for the enacting of our love, or as the lap into which you and your creatures pour the stores of your kindness. But we shall be no longer concerned to enrich or to promote a being which you will have already filled with all the glory it can contain, so that, to be capable of more, we must cease to be the creature you made us.

The third reconciliation is of body and soul. In this life we may often 'delight in your law according to the inner man,' yet we find 'a law in our members making war on the law of our mind and bringing us into subjection.' Unless we give rein to heart and fancy there is a coldness in our virtue, chilling our neighbours and afflicting our minds with barrenness. But if we indulge our nature, it carries us away into bondage, and makes us slaves of that bodily law. Who shall deliver us from our mortal body, which we cannot condemn to death, or we die away ourselves from the roots, nor can we grant it life, or it overpowers us?

Even in this life you begin the redemption of our body. When you move us to love you heartily, and our neighbour for your sake, the very sap of nature is drawn into this love. But what will it be when you have completed our redemption and made the reconciliation indissoluble; when the springs of our nature will be not thinner and cooler, but warmer and more copious than they now are, yet running without reluctance in the channels our mind opens to them? Then no one will ask any more which is the master, body or mind, reason or appetite. For if reason interprets the dumb aspiration of our glorified body it will interpret a true oracle, and if spirit calls on flesh to support its highest flights it will need to exercise no compulsion.

The fourth reconciliation is between the contrary forces of created nature. For in this world most of the things we know by our senses imitate and express the life of their Creator by an unlimited assertion of individual being. Only men and angels so partake of your spiritual likeness as to share in your concern for all things equally, and for the balance of the universe; and we, indeed, most imperfectly, through our addiction to our own bodies. We see universal justice and we pursue the interest of our kind, or of ourselves. We, then, with a measure of guilt, but other creatures innocently, show the inexhaustible fertility of creation by asserting individual existence. And so nothing moves but by the destruction of other things, and everything dies to give another place. The glory of some is the defacement of others and the health of one is another's disease.

In this creation it is as though all things sprang away from you in pursuit of their own being, and trampled one another in the race. But in that new heaven and earth which you have prepared for them, they will return to you in mutual kindness. Here they exercise unlimited power in becoming themselves, but there there will be scope for all their force in ministering to the exploration of your love, and the execution of your counsels. Here through mutual strife the whole creation is subject to frustration; it groans and travails together, waiting for its liberation, when it shall share in the benefits of our adoption, and the redemption of our bodies. Then there shall be neither death nor disease nor adverse accident, nor shutting out of any creature from another's heart.

The final reconciliation is that which is first and the cause of all the rest, the reconciliation of you and your creatures. In this life, though you are the waterhead and we are the stream, we cannot sink back through the spring to find our origin. And though you have come through from your side and placed your life in your creature, this life, which is Jesus Christ, is removed from our sight, and the communion we have with him in the Spirit is but a colony of heaven in our rebellious earth. It is not the disloyalty of my body to my mind that grieves me most, for all the shame that follows sloth and lust; it is the disloyalty of my mind, my very self, to you, the obstinate pride which follows its own devices and suffocates your inspirations. Even so your Son acknowledges me as a part of himself, and counterworks my treason by his suffering love. But what will it be when his love prevails, and by society with him I am made what his love accounts me? How sweet to lose my will and to have yours in perfect liberty; to converse as a son with you, through the Spirit of your Son!

O God, the glories are hidden; we have them by faith and by your word. Believing in you, we believe in your promises. And yet it is not one thing to believe in you, and something additional to believe in what you promise. For it is you that have promised, and if you had not promised, you would not be you; still less, if your promises failed of their fulfilment. For what are you to us, if you are not an Almighty Father, and what Father are you, if you do not bring your children home?

Even now we do not receive your promises as sounds in our ears lacking present effect. For the word and the Spirit by which you assure us of felicity to come are the beginning and foretaste of what they foretell. The order of Grace in which our redemption has placed us is nothing but the fivefold reconciliation beginning to work; our present salvation is a first dawning of heaven. I do not know which of two things I ought to say—that we understand glories not yet possessed by the token of present mercies, or that we understand mysteries obscured in the darkness of our present state through their foreseen manifestation in everlasting light. Or shall I say both things together? For without the present tokens of your love, we should have neither taste nor sense of your glorious promises; and without the promises of glory, we should have no understanding of your present love. For this is your love, that you have taken us by the hand to lead us to yourself; and if you led us blindfold in this darkness without revealing to us the destination of our journey, we should not know in what your love essentially consists. But now we know, because he who is the Way says also that he is the everlasting Life of his friends.

O how amiable are thy dwellings : thou Lord of hosts!

My soul hath a desire and longing to enter into the courts of the Lord : my heart and my flesh rejoice in the Living God.

Yea, the sparrow hath found her an house, and the swallow a nest where she may lay her young : even thine altars, O Lord of hosts, my King and my God.

Blessed are they that dwell in thy house : they will be alway praising thee.

Blessed is the man whose strength is in thee : in whose heart are thy ways;

Who going through the vale of misery use it for a well : and the pools are filled with water.

They will go from strength to strength : and unto the God of gods appeareth every one of them in Sion.

Blessed be God,
Blessed be his holy Name.
Blessed be Jesus Christ, very God and very Man,
Blessed be the holy Name of Jesus;
Blessed be Jesus Christ in the throne of his glory,
Blessed be Jesus Christ in the mystery of the altar.
Blessed be God in his angels and saints,
Blessed be God.

CHAPTER IX

The Heaven-sent aid

THOSE who have troubled to read this book so far have probably been moved by the hope that the exercise would refresh for them the mysteries of faith, so leading them to prayer. They may make it a custom to use a book occasionally for such a purpose, but they will not, perhaps, wish to pray from books as a rule, but to meditate freely on the Scriptures. And if they can do so, it is excellent. But experience shows that free meditation often proves a difficult or almost impossible practice to keep up, and for the benefit of those who find it so, I will conclude with the mention of a well-tried alternative.

If I had been asked two dozen years ago for an example of what Christ forbade when he said 'Use not vain repetitions,' I should very likely have referred to the fingering of beads. But now if I wished to name a special sort of private devotion most likely to be of general profit, prayer on the beads is what I should name. Since my previous opinion was based on ignorance and my present opinion is based on experience, I am not ashamed of changing my mind. Christ did not, in fact, prohibit repetition in prayer, the translation is false; he prohibited gabbling, whether we repeat or whether we do not. Rosaries, like any other prayers, can be gabbled, and if they are gabbled, they certainly will not be profitable. Devout persons who take to the beads as a way of meditating are not likely to gabble, for their object is to meditate.

It may be that as a form of corporate devotion the rosary, recited aloud, is harder not to gabble than more varied forms, such as litanies or the set morning and evening prayer. This is not to deny that it may well be used in public. Those who say it privately may wish sometimes to share it; and how else are we to teach the use of beads to children? However that may be, we are here discussing not corporate recitation, but private meditation.

It may seem disgraceful to commend a method of prayer because it is easy. If we have to choose between the actual performance of an easy task and of one more difficult, the difficult task is probably more worthwhile. Very well, if that is really the choice before us; but often, unfortunately, it is not. Our real choice lies between the performance of an easy task, and the abandonment of a difficult one. It is the most stupid form of pride to refuse to do what we can, when we have learnt from experience that we are too weak to do what we should wish. God desires our love, and we cannot be doing well if we withhold our prayers from him, until we have braced ourselves to some unwonted pitch of concentration; like those conceited conversationalists who will not open their lips to their friends, unless they have twisted their ideas into a knot of epigrams.

How many Christians there must be who, in addition to their ordinary prayers for themselves and their friends, have a somewhat vague intention to spend a certain time nourishing their hearts with the revealed goodness of God. They will read a piece of the Gospel overnight, and pick three points out of it. Next morning they will converse with God about these matters, and so pass on to acts of affection or adoration. And it would be excellent if this were done, but it does not happen. Something interfered with the reading, our attempts to meditate were lost in distraction, we gathered no affection to express in the concluding acts. And so, becoming discouraged, we have banished meditation to the limbo of the things which it would be good to do.

But now a string of beads comes into our hands. Whenever we are doing nothing else, we can use it; if we cannot have the beads on our laps we can finger them in our pockets; our fellow-passengers will be none the wiser. We do not have to find a subject on which to fix our meditation, for the devotion of the rosary supplies us with a chain of scenes impossible to forget, and sufficiently varied to avoid staleness; scenes so well chosen that everything in heaven and earth crowds into them, and so rationally arranged that we pass from one to the next without effort or disturbance. The series runs together into a path, and the path goes through the heart of the country. If I meditate for myself on the text of Scripture I may constantly choose the byways which fit the bias of my mind, and miss the centre of faith. But if I follow the fifteen scenes, or mysteries, of the rosary I shall stick to the beaten track; and I am unlikely to quarrel with the beatenness of it, when I consider whose feet have trodden it.

I can look at each scene, or mystery, long enough to be sure I have it in mind. When I have grasped it, I am not left struggling for the words in which to develop my prayer. Ten times the bead passing through my fingers puts a sweet and familiar speech into my mouth, to address to the person in the scene before me. On the eleventh bead I glorify the Trinity of Persons, and preface the next mystery by addressing the Father in the Lord's Prayer.

The words attaching to the beads serve all the purposes of prayer, and the transition from one use of them to another can take place naturally and without any conscious change of intention. Our first business will probably be to capture the restlessness of the mind by giving it something to do. It must revolve vigorously in a limited space until by spinning it is charmed into quiet. And this is achieved by saying the words with close attention. Our lips may separate every word as our fingers separate every bead; we will not let it go from us until it has had its full weight. The better to hold our attention, the syllables may be actually spoken, though not necessarily with any sound.

But it may not be useful to continue in this way. Perhaps in the first mystery, perhaps in the second or third the mind becomes quiet, and the heart begins to move in affection towards the love of God. Our attention shifts from the words to the mystery in face of which the words are spoken. The use of the formula changes : from being the signpost of our thought it becomes the expression of our affection. Our devotion is sustained and prolonged by having something to say, but does not reflect on what it says; it is happy not to have to find words, but to be supplied with those of the rosary. In the same way, when we greet our friends or give voice to a strongly felt delight, we must say something, but it does not matter what, and we are glad to have the ordinary conventional phrases ready in our mouths; and there is nothing more likely than that we shall repeat them over and over again.

Such liberations of our affection, whatever the affection may be, love, penitence, adoration, are not always at all lasting. The feeling, indeed, is of no importance; but, feeling or no feeling, it would be well if, as we run the beads through our fingers and the prayers through our minds, we could sustain a quiet and devout attention to God, without going aside. But there is no forcing such effects; perhaps our mind wanders or empties. Then all we have to do is to begin saying the words again with careful attention, as we did at first. Never mind, we have prayed as we were able.

If we have to keep up a close attention to the words, there is still no need for us to fall into a dull monotony. Every twelfth bead introduces a new mystery, a fresh scene for contemplation. And even within a single mystery we can vary our attention, at one time centring our consideration on the person to whom we speak, and at another on what we say to, or about the person.

To speak most generally, the difficulty of meditative prayer is to keep hold of the thread and not to stray; and it seems almost too good to be true, that I can have an unbreakable thread, not the gossamer of my ideas but jeweller's beads and wire, between my finger and thumb. Undisciplined as I may be, I can hold on to that, and the words accompany the beads, the mind the words. Since my bodily nature is such a cause of distraction to my soul, let me for once have my revenge upon it, and charge it with the task of steadying my prayer.

I trust it is not necessary to defend the use of the fingers in prayer against the charge of unspirituality. Is it any less spiritual to read the Bible by touch, as the blind do, than to read it by sight, as we do? What is really unspiritual is to perform merely physical routines which employ neither the mind nor the heart, and to suppose that they are in some way meritorious; as if an Oriental monk were to turn a prayer-wheel with one hand while he was throwing dice with the other. Spiritual acts must be the acts of the thinking self. But whether we think with our brains alone or with our tongues and hands, is not a matter of principle; how can we manage best? Jesus has taught us to adore God in taking and breaking, in giving and receiving bread. It seems unnecessary to look for any other authority.

The connection of beads with meditation on Mary is an accident of history. If we find that we can meditate with beads, and without them cannot, that will be a poor reason for meditating on her, and her alone. We must contrive to bring other themes within the scope of the method. About the person of Mary, I cannot have the happiness to know my reader's sentiments, but I can have the generosity to acquit them of a crime. I will not suppose them to hate a name, because others have inordinately loved it.

For whatever reason, the devotion of the rosary has taken shape round the name of Mary. We will pick it up just as it is, and try what we can do to draw it, without violence, into a wider use.

The traditional mysteries of the rosary fall into three groups of five—the joys belonging to Christ's birth, the sorrows belonging to his passion, the glories following upon his resurrection. In the first group we must have a human person other than Jesus himself, with whom to identify our thought. We cannot view the birth, not to name the conception, of Jesus through the eyes of Jesus, but (it is really inevitable) through Mary's. The glories of the third group equally require a witness—we shall scarcely endeavour to enter into the Resurrection, Ascension, and Sending of the Holy Ghost through an exploration of the action and mind of Jesus himself. Mary was only one among those who lived through the glorious mysteries, but, since we have been seeing the joyful mysteries of the nativity through her, it seems worse than pointless to change the person of the witness.

For the joyful mysteries have cemented a unique bond of love between her Son and her, and we desire to follow it to the end; not only through Easter and Pentecost, but on into Mary's death and glory. For he who did not abhor her womb took her to himself in her death, and crowned her with glory in heaven.

The mysteries of the passion hold the middle place, and the need for the figure of a witness is not so evident in them. For in these mysteries Jesus as a grown man comes before us in the state of our earthly condition. To deny that we can enter into the mind of Jesus, or go with him in the endurance of his passion, is to break the bond of the Incarnation and to destroy our holy faith. Not only must the possibility of our doing these things be admitted as a point of theory; we must actually do them. To meditate the passion through the figure of the Redeemer is an essential exercise of the Christian mind. To approach the passion through the figure of any witness, though it be Mary herself, is optional, however edifying. There is no binding reason why we should ever do it. Will it not be better, then, to leave her out of the sorrowful mysteries?

But on the other side of the argument it may be represented as a grievous thing to break the continuity of the threefold series—to go from Mary in the first five to Mary in the last five, but not through Mary in the middle five. We do not wish to lose the middle chapters of Mary's history; and if any one's heart was concerned in the passion, surely hers was.

The dilemma which we have posed is nevertheless artificial. There is no reason why we should not go right through with Mary, if we are so moved. Only not always. It is more vital to identify ourselves with our Redeemer than to share the sympathetic love of any saint.

If the rosary were to remain among the outworks of devotion, it might be tolerable that it should pivot on Mary always. But what is being suggested in this chapter is something different— that the rosary is a heaven-sent aid for those who find it difficult otherwise to meditate on divine mysteries, or contemplate God. If such people take up the rosary, it is going to bulk large in their

meditative prayer. And it is no answer to say that it may not bulk
large in the whole of their private prayer, since intercession and
petition, examination, penitence and resolution will always form
the staple of it. For it will still be a strange thing if we are never
to meditate the love of God in Christ's life and passion, except
through the eyes and heart of Mary. It is true that Mary is
throughout turned towards Jesus. But the Christian has himself
to go on into the heart of Jesus, to see things from there; and he
will not be helped to do so by repeating the Hail Mary, words
which recall him constantly to consider the blessedness of her
grace, and to invoke her prayers both in life and in death.

If, then, the beads are to play a large part in our meditative
prayer, we shall do well to substitute another form for the Hail
Mary in the mysteries of the passion. And, since we must suggest
something, the following prayers are comparable with it in weight
and structure.

> Blessed be Jesus Christ, very God and very Man,
> Blessed be the holy name of Jesus.
> O Saviour of the world, who by thy cross and precious
>   blood hast redeemed us,
> Save us and help us, we humbly beseech thee, O Lord.

Once we are provided with such an alternative formula, we
see that the uses of the rosary are unlimited. If the telling of
beads with a simple repeating prayer is a profitable way to
worship God in the fifteen mysteries, it may be no less profitable
with other objects of contemplation. If we have been meditating
on any passage of the Gospel, we may wish to continue our
adoration by taking up the beads, and saying one or two tens with
such words as we have written just above. Such practices require
no elaborate forethought. If, on the other hand, we venture to
draw up lists of five mysteries for frequent use in addition to the
traditional fifteen, we must be careful to choose scenes which will
bear constant meditation. Perhaps either of these rosaries of
Christ's life might be sometimes used between the rosary of his
birth and that of his passion.

MYSTERIES OF OBEDIENCE

The Baptism	Matt. 3 : 13–17
The Temptation	Matt. 4 : 1–11
The Transfiguration	Matt. 17 : 1–8
The Anointing	Matt. 26 : 6–13
The Supper	Matt. 26 : 20–9

MYSTERIES OF GRACE

Wine	John 2 : 1–11
Water	John 4 : 5–14
Bread	John 6 : 5–35
Light	John 9 : 1–38
Life	John 11 : 14–44

We have commended the rosary as easy to use, in the sense that it provides us with something we can always do there and then. It hardly needs saying that the practice is, nevertheless, worth what we put into it and what it costs us. We must be giving ourselves to the love of God in our prayer, and that is not easy or effortless. Even so the rosary may be too easy for unbroken use, and some of those who make it the staple of their meditative diet will use it better if they sometimes put it aside in favour of a freer and, probably, more difficult sort of meditation. There must be many people for whom it would be sinful laziness not to make this occasional effort, just as there are many people who ought not to allow themselves much use of the rosary at all.

Is there anything which, in conclusion, we can do to enliven the use of the rosary for those who know it, or to introduce it to those who do not? Perhaps both purposes will be served if we write down a single paragraph on each of twenty mysteries, placing it in a certain light.

CHAPTER X
Twenty Mysteries
(1)
MYSTERIES OF JOY

Before each mystery:
Our Father . . . but deliver us from evil. Amen.

With each mystery, ten times:
Hail Mary, full of grace, the Lord is with thee.
Blessed art thou among women
And blessed is the fruit of thy womb, Jesus.
Holy Mary, mother of God, pray for us sinners now and at
the hour of our death.[1] Amen.

After each mystery, once:
Glory be to the Father . . . without end. Amen.

I
Annunciation

Like sunlight in a burning-glass, God's love for us all narrows
to a needle of fire, and pierces Mary at Gabriel's salutation. Her
young heart quivers at the touch, and, when she has reconciled
herself to God's grace, still does not know what it will lay on
her. When she declares herself the handmaid of the Lord, she
enslaves herself to the service of an invisible point which begins
from that moment to be in her; a point of infinite growing-
power, our joy, our love, our immortality, God Only-Begotten.

II
Visitation

God reaches out to God. God's miracle in Mary carries her to
visit her cousin, whom he has blessed already with a kindred
mercy. She goes, and our salvation travels with her; the secret
of incarnate God is folded in her womb. She may seem to carry
him where she pleases; but no one takes God anywhere who is
not sent by Almighty Wisdom. The going is in Mary's feet,
but God directs her heart, and God is the blessing she brings.
She arrives, and the grace in her joins hands with the grace in
Elizabeth; at the sound of Mary's greeting the child of promise
leaps in her cousin's womb.

[1] No Christian is obliged to invoke the prayers of any saint in his
own devotions. For the last sentence those who wish may say: Son of
Mary, Son of the Living God, have mercy on us now and at the hour
of our death. Amen.

III
Nativity

Mary bears Jesus Christ, she sees, caresses, holds him and enjoys him for her own. Jesus is what she was for, his being and happiness are her natural fulfilment, in caring for him she is most herself. Blessed above women is she in whom the pull of nature is one with the drawing of grace; for whom the embracing of her child is the embracing of our only, all-sufficient and everlasting good. God gives us one another as images of his glory, he gives Mary himself as the dear fruit of her womb.

IV
Presentation

Mary and Joseph present the Child in the temple of God. By law, the firstborn son is God's; they pay a ransom to have him with themselves, they borrow him from heaven. But, being lent to them, he is not taken from God; he is dedicated to his heavenly Father. Mary and Joseph offer him there and then; soon he will offer himself, and them along with himself. This is the acceptable sacrifice, the Beloved Son. Ah, Mary, how straight your prayers went when you prayed to be a mother to your Child, and that all things might advance his holy calling.

V
Finding in the Temple

Mary bore Jesus, she suckled and afterwards fed him. She gave him the stuff of his body; the life which built it up was not hers. She gave her Child the matter of his mind; he had no words to think with, but what she had taught him; his first conscious acts were imitations of her own. But the most receptive of sons is no mere piecing together of his mother's thought. He has gone on his own feet into the temple, he questions the doctors out of his own heart. Mary loses the trail, but she must find it, and come up with Jesus where he is. She who taught him must learn to know him. She must find her place in a new world issuing from his will, and promising her many sorrows.

(2)
MYSTERIES OF OBEDIENCE

Before each mystery:
Our Father . . . but deliver us from evil. Amen.

With each mystery, ten times:
Blessed be Jesus Christ, very God and very Man.
Blessed be the holy name of Jesus.
O Saviour of the world, who by thy cross and precious blood
    hast redeemed us,
Save us and help us, we humbly beseech thee, O Lord.

After each mystery, once:
Glory be to the Father . . . without end. Amen.

I
Baptism

John dissuades Jesus from being baptized, but he will not be
dissuaded; he joins his people in dedication for what is to come.
He has no sooner touched the dedicating waters, than it comes;
the skies open, the Spirit like a spark of power flies from the
heart of heaven to his, the Father's voice is in his ears : You are
my beloved Son, he says, in you is my delight.

II
Temptation

You are my Son, says God. And Satan says : If you are his
Son, the power is yours; command the stones to nourish you.
And if you are God's Son, make God declare himself; leap
from this pinnacle, feel the feathered shoulders under your feet.
If you are Son of God, enjoy your inheritance; the kingdoms are
before you; bow to me, and they are yours. Ah no, says Christ;
he is my Father, and I will live on every breath of his utterance.
He is my Father, I will put him to no kind of test. He is my
Father; I bend the knee to no other, and ask no inheritance from
any other will.

III

Transfiguration

Jesus, the healer and teacher of multitudes, turns his face to Jerusalem and death. Before he goes, he climbs high into the hills. He prays, and the cloud touches him. He is transfigured, and what he is, shines out of him. Old saints are visible in his light, conversing with him. It is good to be here; if good for Peter and his companions, how much more blest for Christ, that he should inhabit a mountain hermitage, taken up in God. But men must be illuminated, and from another station; a wooden candlestick on Calvary awaits the light of the world.

IV

Anointing

Resting in a lull between his clash with power and the passover feast, Jesus feels the touch of kindness, the caress of nard, poured by a woman in honour on his head. How can they blame her? It would be a kind thing, certainly, to feed the hungry with her wealth, but it is a kind thing equally to bury the dead; and doubly kind that flesh should feel the outpoured affection before it goes to the grave, insensible of love. Anointing him for burial, she thinks she is anointing him for glory. She is not wrong; he goes to a kingdom.

V

Supper

Christ sits at supper with his friends. One food and drink will become his body and theirs. The life they live will flow from a single cup, a single loaf; a loaf, a cup for which the blessing has been said, making it what it is to be. And what is it to be? Broken bread, wine outpoured; blood shed, a body crucified; the body and blood of the sole redeeming sacrifice, offered by Christ, partaken by his friends.

(3)
MYSTERIES OF GRIEF

Before each mystery:
  Our Father . . . but deliver us from evil. Amen.
With each mystery, ten times:
  Blessed be Jesus Christ, very God and very Man,
  Blessed be the holy name of Jesus.
  O Saviour of the world, who by thy cross and precious blood
    hast redeemed us,
  Save us and help us, we humbly beseech thee, O Lord.
After each mystery, once:
  Glory be to the Father . . . without end. Amen.

I
Sweat of Blood

Jesus in the garden prayed the prayer of nature, asking to live. Finding it unprayable, he consented to die, and such a death. Then the Lord's Prayer became the flesh and blood of the Lord who gave it. Abba, Father, thy kingdom come, and so thy will, not mine, be done. Give daily bread, give it from the altar of the cross. (He who prays has just left the supper-table, and will presently be crucified to make good his sacramental words.) Forgive trespasses, especially to these who sleep, whose flesh is too weak to pray against entering into temptation; who find deliverance in flight, and not in you when, sword in hand, Evil appears.

II
The Lash

The love of God is never words, never sound and breath. His love is Jesus, sent bodily among us, bodily living and dying, bodily risen. And this embodied love of God meets a rejection and hatred which does not stop at words either. No sooner has hatred pronounced the sentence than hatred lays the lashes on. The lashes bring the hatred home and hatred sharpens the sting of the lash. This, he knows with every stripe, this is what they think of me. But love, however lashed, is not driven out. The more it is defenceless, the more it shows itself almighty. He has us at his mercy, having disarmed our rebel hands, now that all our arrows are in his heart.

III
The Crown of Thorns

This is the jest against Jesus, his being what he is, King in the kingdom of God. The crown of his kingdom is firm on his brows, for the thorns go in, and scorn drives them. Scorn forces upon its victim the hateful character it imputes; the scorn of the people, not the hand of the soldier, presses the crown on Jesus' head, identifying him with the mockery of what he is. So torture thrusts on him his joy and his glory, the sovereignty of God, to uphold through all suffering, all contempt. We that have put on the Lord Jesus have put on scorn, to glorify his crown in every place.

IV
The Cross

We shake it off, but Christ shoulders it, the cross, a burden not chosen but imposed and accepted. Among a world of men giving way where the load rubs them, Jesus takes the rub and carries the cross. It breaks his skin, it bites into his shoulder, but he carries it. What does he carry? He carries us all, for we who do not do our part in carrying drag on what he carries. What does he carry? He carries the dead weight of the world; he stands against the avalanche of cowardice and evasion, and when he is crushed to death under the weight, Father, he says, forgive them, for they know not what they do.

V
The Nails

The self-offering of the Son to his Father and his brethren is made absolute at last, and put beyond the possibility of recall. It began with acceptance, but it becomes necessity; our victim is nailed up alive immovable, incorporated with the dead wood. He is dragged through the breakdown of the body to the breaking of the mind, of which the last fragments and leavings are verses from the psalms : My God, my God, why hast thou forsaken me?—Father, into thy hands I commend my spirit.

(4)
MYSTERIES OF GLORY

Before each mystery:
  Our Father . . . but deliver us from evil. Amen.
With each mystery, ten times:
  Hail Mary, full of grace, the Lord is with thee.
  Blessed are thou among women
  And blessed is the fruit of thy womb, Jesus.
  Holy Mary, mother of God, pray for us sinners now and at
    the hour of our death.[1] Amen.
After each mystery, once:
  Glory be to the Father . . . without end. Amen.

I
Resurrection

Mary has seen Jesus crucified. The sword is in her heart, horror before her eyes; dawn wakes her to a blank of grief. They say, His tomb is empty—there are sentry angels—Magdalen has seen him—he is risen indeed, has shown himself to Simon; and on the heels of the message he stands himself among his friends. His mother lives again. She cannot keep him, but he is happy, and one world of love embraces them both. Only she wishes she still might live her life for him. Reflection tells her that she may, for on the cross he said to her 'Woman, behold thy son.' John took her home, and in serving him she will serve her Son. For, risen and glorified, Christ lives in his followers.

II
Ascension

Christ is gone up. The mystical body extends, through Christ its head, to embrace the very life of God in God. Mary, lifting her hands among the disciples, prays in Jesus' words, in Jesus' mind. What she asks is what he asks, it is asked by God from God. The prayer of her love is a movement of the heart in the Blessed Trinity, it is the converse between the divine Persons, the asking and granting of filial desire. And so it is, when at one with Mary and all saints, we pray in Jesus' name.

[1] *Or:* Son of Mary, Son of the Living God, have mercy on us now and at the hour of our death. Amen.

III

Pentecost

The body of mankind extends upward into God, the life of God descends into the body of mankind. The Spirit comes down to be the inspiration of divine desires, the life of the self we are through Jesus. Mary is wrapped in fire and burns in flame towards heaven; the love with which she cares, the hope by which she aspires, the joy in which she exults, are the kindling of a fuel Christ laid in order, by fire fallen from God.

IV

Taking up

The bond of the Incarnation is unbreakable, and Mary, dying, is united with her Son. He came from her womb, she goes into his mystical body; once she was home for him, now he is home to her. She surrenders to him the flesh from which he had his own. He takes up the pieces where she lays them down and remakes her life in the stuff of glory. He cherishes the dear familiar body, entirely her own in every part, and entirely the work of his hands.

V

Crown of Life

Mary is crowned with the diadem of life, her height of degree in the happy-making vision of God. When Simeon had feasted his eyes on God's salvation he was willing to depart, but what Mary sees will never let her go. For though God be Spirit and invisible to sense, he is perfectly known in infinite actions. No word, no gesture, no conduct ever betrayed love to love as God's heart is laid open in the whole state and life of heaven. His unveiled countenance is the whole face of things, and the eyes are Jesus Christ, God seeing and visible.